Roses

and Rose Gardens

Roses
and Rose Gardens

Claire Masset

National Trust

Previous page *The armillary sundial in the second rose garden at Mottisfont, Kent.* **Right** *Rosa 'Ambroise Paré'.*

First published in the United Kingdom in 2019 by
National Trust Books
43 Great Ormond Street
London WC1N 3HZ
An imprint of Pavilion Books Company Ltd

ISBN: 9781911358688

A CIP catalogue record for this book is available from the British Library.

25 24 23 22 21 20 19
10 9 8 7 6 5 4 3 2 1

Reproduction by Rival Colour Ltd, UK
Printed and bound by 1010 Printing International Ltd, China

This book can be ordered direct from the publisher at the website: www.pavilionbooks.com, or try your local bookshop.

CONTENTS

INTRODUCTION 6

THE STORY OF THE ROSE 12

ROSES FOR EVERY GARDEN 26
Rose Types 28
Perfect Partners 52
Reaching New Heights 62

CLASSIC ROSE GARDENS 70
Bateman's 72
Borde Hill Garden 75
Broughton Castle 78
Cliveden 82
Coughton Court 86
David Austin Roses 106

Helmingham Hall 112
Hever Castle and Gardens 116
Kiftsgate Court 120
Mottisfont 122
Peckover 136
Queen Mary's Rose Garden 138
RHS Rosemoor 142
Sissinghurst Castle Garden 144

SIMPLE ROSE CARE 166

Further Reading 172
Picture Credits 173
Index 174
Acknowledgements 176

INTRODUCTION

I saw the sweetest flower wild nature yields,
A fresh-blown musk-rose; 'twas the first that threw
Its sweets upon the summer: graceful it grew
As is the wand that queen Titania wields.

JOHN KEATS,
'TO A FRIEND WHO SENT ME
SOME ROSES', 1884

Roses have held me under their spell ever since I was a young girl. Each of my childhood gardens recalls pictures rich with the scent and spectacle of these summer gems. At my family home in France, my father spent the weekends tending his plot on the outskirts of Paris, where lavender, lavatera and roses took centre stage in June and July. One of my most vivid memories of the garden is a long-lasting display of small bright blooms, from what I now think was probably *Rosa* 'Crimson Shower' (top left). Each year it would cover the garden wall with its red and green cloak, prolific sprays pouring into our neighbour's garden with abandon.

Enjoying a quietly creative retirement, my maternal grandfather designed a small rose bed in his Sussex garden, filling it with proud hybrid teas and the towering 'Queen Elizabeth'. It stood in front of the patio and was the backdrop to many a happy family gathering. Behind us, *Rosa* 'Albertine' warmed the red-brick walls of the house, its salmon-pink blooms like frilly tutus in the eyes of my ballet-loving young self.

On my thirteenth birthday, my paternal grandmother handed me a black plastic pot with a few twigs sticking from it. I stared at the label attached and beamed: *Rosa* 'Iceberg' (top right), it said. Here in my hands was the promise of the most beautiful white rose. The thought that this plant would be mine, all mine, in a garden that was very much my father's domain, was thrilling. I waited six months for it to flower, but flower it did, gloriously, copiously, endlessly. I was enraptured.

It was not until I was 28 that I acquired my own garden, at the time little more than a waste ground with years of work ahead of it. The front garden was my starting point. Here I planted my first rose. There it still flowers today; a much-loved and much-admired 'Jacques Cartier' (bottom left). It is the most reliable rose you could wish for – the perfect choice for a beginner. Each richly scented flower has the sweetest little button eye. It really is a charmer, and great in a vase too.

As my garden slowly took shape, I pored over catalogues, pondering which roses to buy and dreaming of a larger plot (but grateful for its rich Cotswold soil). All the while I worried that I would not be 'up to the job' of looking after these delicate jewels. I have since realised that roses are pretty easy to grow. My *Rosa rugosa* 'Rubra' is pure joy. I give it very little attention and it repays my neglect with large, cheerful and sweet-smelling flowers from late May to the very end of summer. I have discovered that 'Gertrude Jekyll' really is the most magnificent and hardy of all English Roses, a queen among so many princesses. And I treasure my lovely 'Ballerina' (bottom right); its dainty apple-blossom blooms spreading delight throughout the season.

But I have learned lessons along the way. Mostly that roses do not like to be too dry or overcrowded and cannot cope with too much shade. On one of my many catalogue-scouring evenings, I fell in love with *Rosa* 'Maiden's Blush'. The name on its own would have been enough for me, but its delicate pale pink flowers sealed my decision. I had just the spot for it, I thought, as I envisioned it embellished by the tendrils and trumpet flowers of my Japanese honeysuckle, glowing in a dark corner of the garden. Alba roses, I read, do not mind shade, so I rejoiced. No need to worry with this rose! It would be happy in its sombre spot. And indeed it was, for quite a while. But I let the rampant honeysuckle take over, did not weed or feed my rose, and eventually paid the price. Now I know that there a few simple rules for rose care. Follow these (which are described at the back of the book) and you will be fine.

This is not, however, a 'how-to' gardening book. It is a celebration of our best-loved flower: its long history and rich symbolism; the beauty and diversity of its flowers, foliage and habits; its wonderful fragrances; and, above all, its amazing versatility. There are roses for every plot and spot – from formal beds and mixed borders to patios and containers, fences and walls, and even wild areas such as orchards and meadows. Perhaps the most precious quality of the rose is that (if properly looked after!) it will happily coexist with other plants, offering endless opportunities for attractive and atmospheric combinations in your garden.

I hope you will find lots of inspiration for your own garden in this book. In the series of rose portraits, I describe the individual quality of each rose – what I think makes it a good choice and where you can grow it and give suggestions on how you might combine it with other plants. I also explore some of our best-loved rose gardens, for there is nothing like seeing roses in the flesh to get a sense of their true natures. Hardened rose spotters will tell you that almost every garden you visit has at least one rose in it. So explore at your leisure and enjoy the thrill of discovering new varieties each year?

As my grandmother knew, there is nothing like the gift of a rose. For my mother's retirement, I bought her *Rosa* 'Escapade' (right) – a floriferous floribunda with pale lilac-pink flowers and a fitting name for someone who was escaping the world of work and hoping for fresh adventures. This rose has now travelled with her from our old family garden to her new flat and happily flowers in a pot on the patio. Roses are not just things of great beauty. They have the power to carry meaning and express emotion, which is why we love them so much – and why Keats and so many other poets were inspired to eulogise about them.

THE STORY
OF THE ROSE

The Rose (mankind will all agree)
The Rose the queen of flowers should be;
The pride of plants, the grace of bowers.
The bush of meads, the eye of flowers ...

ATTRIBUTED TO SAPPHO

Roses are captivatingly mysterious. Fossils bearing their delicate imprint dating back 35 million years are witness to the plant's extraordinary longevity, but where and when roses first blossomed, no one will ever know.

Written records are scant, artistic evidence open to doubt. Knossos in Crete lays the claim for the earliest certain representation of a rose. Painted 3,500 years ago, the Blue Bird Fresco, discovered by British archaeologist Sir Arthur Evans in the 1920s, features a five-petalled rose, now identified as the little-known pine-scented rose, *Rosa pulverulenta*. The plant, native to this part of the Mediterranean, still grows in Crete today.

In 500BC China, the philosopher Confucius remarked on the hundreds of books on roses in the King's library and noted the roses growing in the royal gardens. China was, and indeed still is, a hotspot for roses; over half of the world's 150 or so wild-rose species originate from this country.

Two-hundred years later in Ancient Greece, Theophrastus, the 'Father of Botany', made the first botanical description of roses in his *Enquiry into Plants*. He meticulously recorded their varying characteristics, writing: 'Among roses there are many differences, in the number of petals, in roughness, in beauty of colour, and in sweetness of scent.'

Roses had many functions in ancient times. They appeared in perfume, cosmetics, food, medicine and wine; their petals were used as confetti for celebrations and their flowers worn as wreaths and made into garlands that were later found in ancient tombs.

Whether decorative, culinary or devotional, it seems roses have always been a symbol of love. The Ancient Greeks and Romans associated the flower with their respective goddesses of love, Aphrodite and Venus. Cleopatra was said to have covered her bedroom floor with rose petals to seduce Mark Antony. The rose's great powers of association have continued ever since. Throughout history, it has been an emblem of purity and faith, romance and lust, wisdom and perfection.

Rose cultivation was so widespread in the Roman Empire that by the fall of Rome in AD476, there were at least 2,000 rose gardens across its lands. The Romans grew entire fields of the single-petalled *Rosa gallica*, native to southern and central Europe. A cultivated version, *Rosa gallica* var. *officinalis* (right), made its way to France in the thirteenth century, allegedly introduced by knights returning from the crusades. Throughout medieval Europe, it started appearing in monastery gardens thanks to its medicinal qualities and duly became known as the apothecary's rose.

Few records testify to the use of cultivated roses in the medieval period, but by the sixteenth and seventeenth centuries key works account for their growing prominence. In 1563 Thomas Hill published one of the first popular gardening books in English, *The Profitable Arte of Gardening*, in which he describes how to plant and look after roses. Three decades later, gardener and herbalist John Gerard wrote his great *Herball* (1597), which includes 14 different types of rose, from the most prized of garden roses to humble wild species, to which he devotes a whole chapter.

Focus gradually shifted from the recording of roses solely for their medicinal uses to the inclusion of their botanical and aesthetic features. Such was the work of John Parkinson, apothecary to King James I, whose monumental *Paradisi in Sole Paradisus Terrestris* (1629) describes in detail 24 different roses, including the 'Double Yellow Rose', 'Musk Rose', 'Damask Rose' and 'Carnation Rose'. Parkinson considered roses to be so valuable that he called for a whole book to be written on them.

The tulip notoriously held the botanical centre stage in the seventeenth century, as vast sums of money changed hands for single bulbs, but the financial opportunities offered from creating new roses did not go unnoticed by the canny Dutch growers. Between 1600 and 1720, they introduced almost 200 new roses by means of cross-pollination, including the honey-scented *Rosa × centifolia* (left). The exuberant floral art of the time, such as works by Jan van Huysum, Jan Davidszoon. de Heem and Rachel Ruysch, celebrates the beauty and diversity of a great many flowers. But while the popularity of some of them – hyacinths, hollyhocks, tulips, fritillaries – waxed and waned, the rose remained a constant in these paintings. Its prominence has never ceased. It seems that like a true classic, the rose is immune to the whims of fashion.

Nor has the representation of roses – whether botanical or artistic – ever stopped. Little remembered today, English artist Mary Lawrance blended both forms in her book, *A Collection of Roses from Nature* (1799). This three-year project saw her produce 91 plates, etched and coloured by herself, depicting a great variety of roses. The frontispiece is a glorious garland of roses. Here, finally, was the book John Parkinson had called for.

It is, however, the botanical illustrator Pierre-Joseph Redouté – no doubt thanks to the patronage of none other than Marie-Antoinette and Empress Joséphine – who is remembered today as *the* painter of roses. In *Les Roses*, published in three volumes (1817–24), he illustrates over 160 different types of rose, two of which are attributed to Joséphine's famous garden at Malmaison on the outskirts of Paris. Redouté created his exquisite flower portraits using a technique known as stipple engraving, which involves using tiny dots and allows for much subtlety and detail. The resulting effect, hand-finished in watercolour, is both luminous and delicate.

Empress Joséphine, the first wife of Napoleon I, is history's most famous rose grower. Hers was, according to legend, the first garden dedicated to the cultivation of different roses. With the help of noted botanists and an

Left *Prized for its large, pure pink flowers and the sweetness of its scent, Rosa x centifolia was the most popular rose amongst Dutch growers and artists of the seventeenth century. Its name comes from the abundance of its petals.*

army of gardeners, she is said to have grown over 250 different types of rose on her vast 700-acre (283ha) plot. Joséphine paved the way for the Victorian fascination with roses and rose gardens, but she certainly did not do so single-handedly. Concurrent developments were helping to spread the plant's popularity.

Chief among these was the introduction of Chinese roses to the West from the late eighteenth century. The most famous were the so-called Stud Chinas: 'Slater's Crimson China' (1792), 'Parsons' Pink China' (1793), 'Hume's Blush Tea-scented China' (1809) and 'Parks' Yellow Tea-scented China' (1824). Perhaps their greatest asset was that they, and other Chinese roses, bloomed for a much longer season than their European counterparts. By crossing them with other roses, breeders were able to create new repeat-flowering hybrids. No longer were roses a flower just for the summer.

As roses become more widespread, so too did books on their cultivation. One of the most influential works on the subject was *The Rose Garden* (1848) by horticulturist William Paul. An exhaustive and practical guide, by 1903 it had reached its tenth edition. Another seminal work was Samuel Reynold Hole's *A Book about Roses: How to grow and show them* (1869) in which he extols the virtues of 'the Queen of Flowers'. It subtitle reflects his fascination for growing show roses. Hole was, after all, the founder of the National Rose Society (1876) which, as well as undertaking trials of new varieties, advocated for roses to be judged at events. He organised the first National Rose Show, held in St James's Hall, London, on 1 July 1858, which drew in over 2,000 visitors. Each exhibition rose was shown as a cut flower in small groups. Flowers were judged on their individual blooms and how they looked as a set. Just two years later, the third National Rose Show attracted a crowd of 16,000 people. Local rose societies quickly followed suit and soon smaller shows were taking place across the United Kingdom.

Apart from bringing the rose to the attention of a wider public, shows were designed to celebrate plants with the very best flowers. Breeders competed to bring the largest, most conspicuous blooms to market and avid growers raced to acquire them. To some extent these shows were responsible for spreading the idea that roses were best not mixed with other plants. The way to appreciate a rose, many believed, was to focus on individual specimens. This notion reflected the popular contemporary design concept known as the Gardenesque, introduced by John Claudius Loudon in 1832.

Following what he called the 'Principle of Recognition', he defined the term as 'garden design which is best calculated to display the individual beauty of trees, shrubs and plants'.

Very broadly, Victorian rose gardens consisted of a discrete area within a larger garden: a dedicated space where each plant could be properly appreciated and, crucially, kept neat and tidy. Shirley Hibberd, the most popular garden writer of the Victorian era, summed up the idea in *The Amateur's Rose Book* (1874): 'A rosarium worthy of the name is a good feature in a garden, and, as a rule, will prove to be the most popular of all distinct features.' The rose garden was indeed a separate entity: it even had its own name.

Not everyone agreed, however, and by the end of the Victorian era change was afoot. Gardener and journalist William Robinson wrote that roses 'should be everywhere in the garden where they would grow. We cannot have too many Roses, or Roses in too many places.' His more famous contemporary, Gertrude Jekyll, complained: 'We are growing impatient of the usual rose garden, generally a sort of target of concentric rings of beds placed upon turf, often with no special aim at connected design.' In *Roses for English Gardens* (1902), she describes the many ways in which roses can be enjoyed in the garden: trained up pillars,

Right *The perfect rose to cloak a large tree, 'Blush Rambler' will grow up to 8m (26¼ft). Here it is clambering up one of the old apple trees in the orchard at Sissinghurst Castle Garden in Kent.*

pergolas and arches (see left and following page), grown as hedges, against walls and summer-houses, within a mixed plant border, but also – for those roses with a 'wild way of growth' – clambering up trees and shrubs. Her gardening philosophy argued for greater naturalism and an aesthetic approach. Jekyll had trained as an artist and believed that gardening was a fine art. 'Planting ground is painting a landscape with living things,' she wrote.

Jekyll's influence was long-lasting and still reverberates today. One figure she affected directly was Graham Stuart Thomas. In the early 1930s, while working as a young foreman for Hillings Nursery in Surrey, Thomas sent Jekyll, who lived nearby, a letter of introduction. This resulted in an invitation from the *grande dame* of gardening and a tour of her famous garden at Munstead Wood. She soon became something of a mentor to Thomas, who was concurrently developing a passion for old roses.

Because they only flowered once a year, these roses were under threat from their more floriferous younger cousins, particularly the floribundas and hybrid teas (see page 40). As well as working for the National Trust as an influential gardens adviser, Thomas dedicated his life to saving old roses from extinction. He established an outstanding collection, now housed at Mottisfont in Hampshire (see page 122), and helped bring them back into commercial use. His three books *The Old Shrub Roses* (1955), *Shrub Roses of Today* (1962) and *Climbing Roses Old and New* (1965) effectively made old roses fashionable again. These words in particular sum up his attitude: 'A criticism which is often levelled against old roses is that they only flower once at midsummer. But most of our most loved shrubs, such as forsythia, rhododendrons, philadelphus and lilacs are likewise only once flowering. This is a point to put across to the unconverted.'

In the mid-twentieth century, rose mania reached something of a peak, as membership of the National Rose Society doubled from 45,000 in 1955 to 90,000 in 1960. Roses were accessible to all: you could buy the latest hybrid tea from your local garden centre or department store, rather than searching it out in the mail-order catalogue of a specialist nursery. Novelty roses – with blooms in new and unusual shades of pink, peach, yellow, orange and more – were popular amongst certain rose collectors, many of whom still preferred planting them in neat beds separate from other plants. The hybrid tea, called 'Peace', exemplifies this trend. Its large, upright blooms are creamy-yellow edged with pink (interestingly, its colour varies depending on the soil and climate in which it is grown). For some, it is a duo-tone monster, its large, angular head held proud on a stiff neck. For others it is the most beautiful rose in the world – it was awarded this prestigious title by rose lovers who cast a vote for it in 1976.

While new types and colours were being introduced at increasing pace, two growers followed Graham Stuart Thomas's lead and focused on collecting and developing roses with old-fashioned features. Peter Beales, who had worked with Thomas at Hillings, opened his nursery in 1968. Still today, it is one of the most respected rose sellers in Britain, with an outstanding selection of old and species roses. It is, however, his rival David Austin who has made the strongest impact. A hatred for hybrid teas spurred this young Midlands farmer to create an entirely new family of award-winning roses. World-famous, David Austin's English roses (see page 106) combine the beauty and scent of old roses with the repeat-flowering nature of their more modern counterparts. Every year his nursery introduces new varieties, under the expert eye of the company's technical director, Michael Marriott. According to him, an English rose must above all possess charm – that elusive quality to which it is so easy to succumb.

Today about 3,000 rose varieties are commercially available in the United Kingdom and over 14,000 worldwide. There are roses for all kinds of gardeners, even those without a garden. And while there will always be a market for novelty roses, the trend towards naturalistic planting makes the wild allure of species roses (far right) highly desirable to the modern gardener. Single-flowered roses – particularly attractive to pollinating insects – appeal to our growing ecological awareness. Repeat-flowering roses may be practical, but this advantage now seems less of a draw than a plant's graceful habit, health and hardiness, or even its out-of-season appeal. From the autumnal shades of its leaves, to the brightness of its hips (bottom left) and the sometimes unusual colour of its stems, a rose is, after all, more than just a pretty flower.

Rosa moyesii

Rosa moyesii is one of the most striking of all species roses. Wild gardener and journalist William Robinson was right when he described it as 'the most startlingly beautiful wild rose'.

Introduced to Europe from China in the early twentieth century, it was immediately popular. Rose lover and one-time owner of Sissinghurst Vita Sackville-West adored it: 'If ever a plant reflected all that we had ever felt about the delicacy, lyricism and design of a Chinese drawing, *Rosa moyesii* is that plant ... Three weeks sees her through her explosion of beauty. But her beauty is such that she must be grown for the sake of those three weeks in June. During that time her branches will tumble with the large, single, rose-red flower of her being.'

It is these blood-red flowers that sets *Rosa moyesii* apart from other species roses: endearingly simple, single blooms with heart-shaped petals and a crown of gold and black stamens, offset by attractive grey-green foliage. Second only to the flowers are the much longer-lasting hips that make their bountiful appearance in August. At least 4cm (1½in) long, flask-shaped, bright orange-red, they hang gracefully from arching stems like Christmas-tree decorations.

The only downside is the shrub's size – it is large – so make sure you have room for it. In the autumn its colouring and hips will complement hot schemes of oranges and reds (try it with the dark-leaved *Dahlia* 'Bishop of Oxford' and *Berberis thunbergii*), or purples and lavender-blues such as *Aster × frikartii* 'Mönch', *Buddleja* 'Lochinch' and *Cotinus coggygria* 'Royal Purple'.

Flower | Deep crimson, single, 6cm (2¼in) across
Habit | Large, arching shrub
Average height and spread | 4 x 4m (13 x 13ft)
Flowering | Once in midsummer
Scent | Light
Aspect | Sun or part shade
Type | Species rose

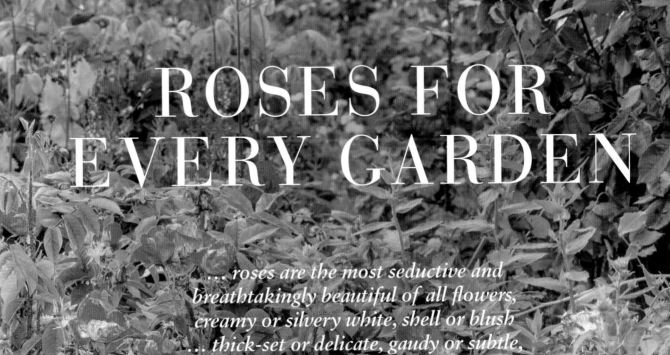

ROSES FOR EVERY GARDEN

*… roses are the most seductive and
breathtakingly beautiful of all flowers,
creamy or silvery white, shell or blush
… thick-set or delicate, gaudy or subtle,
blowsy or modest.*

SUSAN HILL,
THROUGH THE GARDEN GATE, 1986

ROSE TYPES

Rose classification is a complicated affair and one that still causes much debate. Unless you want to start breeding your own roses, this is best left to the experts.

An awareness of the different rose types available and their characteristics can help you decide which to choose for your own garden. Rosarians broadly sort roses into three groups: species, old and modern roses.

SPECIES ROSES

These are the wild or pure roses from which all others originate. The simple beauty of their single, mostly five-petalled blooms is hard to resist and, although they flower only once in early summer, they are followed by a crop of colourful hips. Tough and problem free, and often large, species roses are perfect for wilder areas of the garden. There are hundreds to choose from, with colours for every taste. The most common European wild rose is the much-loved dog rose (*Rosa canina*) of our hedgerows and woodlands. Its early blooming pink or white flowers are always a cheering sight and a sign that summer is finally on its way. The low-growing Scotch rose, *Rosa pimpinellifolia* (right), makes ideal ground cover; it has small creamy-white flowers and near-black hips. Commonly found in wild coastal areas, unlike most roses it is quite happy growing in nutrient-poor, sandy soil.

OLD ROSES

Despite the complexity of rose classification, there is one very simple rule: any rose that came into existence before 1867 is known as an old rose. This was the year when the first ever hybrid tea, known as 'La France', was introduced. But here is the complication: not all roses introduced after 1867 are modern roses. Old roses can be introduced after that date, as long as they belong to an old rose group, such as the ones listed in the following pages. So, for instance, the Bourbon rose 'La Reine Victoria', created in 1872, is an old rose. Old roses can be extremely ancient; many others date from the nineteenth century.

Previous page *The huge lavender-blue globes of Allium cristophii offer a wonderfully muted counterpoint to the luminous, clear pink blooms of Rosa 'Complicata' in the walled rose garden at Mottisfont, Hampshire.* Right *Rosa pimpinellifolia, commonly known as the Scotch rose, is a hardy species rose that will thrive even in poor soil. This low-growing shrub is distinguished by masses of prickles, small, highly decorated leaves and creamy-white flowers. Later in the season, it produces striking maroon-black hips.*

Albas

This ancient group, possibly introduced by the Romans, derives from a cross between the damask rose, *Rosa × damascena*, and the European native dog rose, *Rosa canina*. Shrubs have an upright habit and attractive grey-green foliage. The delicately fragrant double or semi-double flowers are limited to pale pinks and whites and appear in a single flush in midsummer. With strong growth, few thorns and good disease resistance, these elegant roses are worth growing. 'Maiden's Blush' (top left) is particularly appealing – both for its evocative name and its muddled pink petals.

Bourbons

First recorded in 1824, Bourbons came about thanks to a chance cross on the Île de Bourbon (now the island of Réunion) between the autumn damask (*Rosa × damascena* var. *semperflorens*) and the old blush China (*Rosa chinensis*). The result was a rose with large double flowers, a delicious scent and vigorous growth that blooms in both summer and autumn. With its blowsy crimson-pink flowers and attractive foliage 'Madame Isaac Péreire' (see page 94) is a popular choice, but 'Zigeunerknabe' (also known as 'Gipsy Boy') (bottom left), boasting purple blooms and lovely golden anthers, is also recommended.

Centifolias

Derived from the cabbage or 'Provence' rose (*Rosa × centifolia*), centifolias developed thanks to the work of Dutch breeders in the seventeenth century and appear in all their floral glory in many Dutch still lifes of the time. Although the flowers are sumptuous and fragrant, centifolias are not particularly pest and disease resistant and their lax habit means they need some supporting. But who could resist the pale pink charms of 'Petite de Hollande' (top right)?

Chinas

China roses are very different from their European counterparts. The shrubs are more delicate, the stems thinner and the foliage sparser and daintier. They are also more tender, needing protection from the extremes of both summer and winter. The flowers – either single or double – are repeat-flowering and often borne in clusters. The graceful *Rosa × odorata* 'Mutabilis' (bottom right) has delicate paper-like flowers that change colour as they age: from buff-yellow to salmon-pink and crimson.

Damasks

Popular in the Classical world, damasks probably made their way to Europe from the Middle East thanks to the Crusaders. Their strong fragrance is what sets them apart, but the delicate pink or white semi to double flowers are also charming, as are their arching stems and elegant leaves. Raspberry-ripple 'Leda' (top left) is one of the best once-flowering damasks. Repeat-flowering varieties, such as 'Quatre Saisons', derive from the autumn damask (*Rosa × damascena* var. *semperflorens*). 'Quatre Saisons' is one of the oldest roses in cultivation, possibly going as far back as the fifth century BC and mentioned by Herodotus.

Gallicas

Some of the oldest known roses are gallicas, including the apothecary's rose (*Rosa gallica* var. *officinalis*) and *Rosa gallica* 'Versicolor' (commonly known as *Rosa mundi*, see page 98). All originate from the wild rose, *Rosa gallica*, a native of southern and eastern Europe. They form compact shrubs, no higher than 1.2m (4ft), with mostly double flowers, ranging from pale pink to crimson and deepest maroon and flowering once in summer. 'Tuscany Superb' (top right) is one of the showiest of all gallicas. Because of the texture of its crimson petals, it is also known as the Old Velvet Rose.

Hybrid Perpetuals

Developed in the mid-nineteenth century, hybrid perpetuals resulted from the crossing of different types of old rose, including Bourbons and the repeat-flowering China roses. Victorians loved their large blooms and abundant June flowering. It was only when the hybrid teas came on to the scene later in the century that hybrid perpetuals lost their popularity. Many are tall growing and have lanky stems, making them ideal for growing as pillar roses or climbers. Winding them around pillars or arching over the stems and pegging them down deals very well with their tendency to otherwise become very lanky and only flower at their tips. Flowers are restricted to shades of white, pink and red. 'Ferdinand Pichard' (bottom left) is a striking example, with joyous pale pink blooms streaked and splashed with crimson.

Moss Roses

The unusual and utterly charming moss rose is a mutation of the Provence rose, *Rosa × centifolia*. Characterised by a mossy fragrant growth on its stems and sepals, its curious appearance made it popular with the Victorians, who delighted in creating little moss rose posies, some of which carried messages of love. Moss roses produce double flowers, with colours ranging from white to deep crimson. The common moss or old pink moss, *Rosa × centifolia* 'Muscosa' (bottom right), has highly scented pink blooms; it is a summer-flowering variety.

Previous page The pale pink, repeat-flowering China rose 'Irène Watts' lines the walk in the formal Rose Garden at Pashley Manor Gardens in East Sussex. **Top left** *The delicate little damask rose 'Leda', also known as 'Painted Damask'.* **Top right** *A very popular gallica, 'Tuscany Superb' boasts striking golden stamens and rich velvety petals.* **Bottom right** *Like Rosa x centifolia 'Muscosa', all moss roses have a characteristic mossy growth on their sepals.* **Bottom left** *Healthy and repeat-flowering, the hybrid perpetual 'Ferdinand Pichard' is considered one of the best parti-coloured roses.*

Noisettes

Hailing from North America, the sweetly scented noisettes evolved in the early nineteenth century and are the result of a cross between an old blush China rose (*Rosa × odorata* 'Pallida') and a musk rose (*Rosa moschata*). Most are white, cream or pale pink and repeat-flower well. 'Blush Noisette' (top left) produces masses of semi-double pale pink blooms with a rich clove-like fragrance. Like most noisettes, it has lax stems and so is best trained as a climber, reaching up to 3m (10ft) in height. It flowers for an exceptionally long time.

Portlands

Upright and compact, and with highly scented repeat-flowering double blooms, Portlands are a great choice for the small garden. The first 'Portland' was *Rosa paestana*, an imported cross between an autumn damask and a gallica, which was part of the botanical collection of Lady Margaret, Duchess of Portland, in the late eighteenth century. It quickly became known as the Portland rose, with all subsequent varieties developed from this one. *Rosa* 'Jacques Cartier' and 'Comte de Chambord' (see pages 38–39) are popular choices for lovers of rich pink blooms. 'Pergolèse' (top right) is equally appealing; its splendid flowers – a purple-crimson fading to lilac-mauve at the edges – are offset by attractive dark green leaves.

Rugosas

Vigorous and problem free, rugosas are the tough guys of the rose world. All originate from the Japanese rose, *Rosa rugosa*, which grows wild in Asia and Siberia. They form large dense shrubs – ideal for growing as hedges – and have large, repeat-flowering single or double blooms, which are wonderfully scented. The leathery, highly veined leaves are distinctive and often turn golden in the autumn, while the flowers produce showy round hips. Rugosas are ideal for a seaside garden, as they grow well in sandy soils and don't mind exposed sites or salt spray. 'Roseraie de l'Hay' (bottom left) boasts large and fragrant crimson-purple flowers set against a pea-green and exceptionally healthy foliage.

Teas

Rosa odorata – the original tea rose – was crossed with other roses in the 1800s to create deliciously scented, large, semi to double blooms with excellent repeat-flowering qualities. Unfortunately most of these new tea roses were tender and delicate, making them particularly difficult to grow in northern climes. Crossed with the hardier hybrid perpetuals, they produced the reliable hybrid teas. Because of their delicate nature, few tea roses remain commercially available. The blowsy apricot-yellow 'Lady Hillingdon' (bottom right) is one of the most reliable, if you can grow it in a warm and protected spot. It is mostly available as a climber. Many of the tea roses were originally grown in conservatories and this can still be a good way of displaying them now.

Top left *'Blush Noisette', also known as 'Noisette Carnée'.* **Top right** *'Pergolèse', a charming Portland rose, whose blooms sometimes display an elegant green carpel.* **Bottom right** *'Lady Hillingdon', whose flowers start a rich amber and fade to cream.* **Bottom left** *Tough and healthy, rugosas such as 'Roseraie de l'Hay' are useful if you are looking for ease of maintenance, long-lasting flowers and autumn hips.*

Comte de Chambord

Compact and characterful, 'Comte de Chambord' is a must for the small garden where it will happily flower from June until the first frosts. It is one of the first Portlands to bloom and one of the finest, even surpassing its attractive light pink rival, 'Jacques Cartier'.

'Comte de Chambord' boasts large, fully double, strongly scented blooms of a gorgeous clear pink. Its lively petals are densely packed and elegantly quartered, curving inwards at the edges. The healthy foliage is an attractive grey-green.

Tough and reliable and needing no support, this small upright shrub will thrive in the mixed border, where it works hard for its money. Thanks to its long flowering season it will mingle with June-flowering plants, including hardy geraniums, nepetas and campanulas, and enhance such autumn beauties as lavender-blue *Caryopteris* × *clandonensis* 'Dark Knight' and *Perovskia* 'Blue Spire'. As with all Portlands, it is also ideal for growing in containers, so you don't even need a garden to enjoy it.

A cross between the hybrid perpetual *Rosa* 'Baronne Prévost' and the Portland rose, 'Comte de Chambord' was introduced in France in 1863. The original Comte de Chambord (1820–83) – the wonderfully named Henri Charles Ferdinand Marie Dieudonné d'Artois – was heir to the French throne but king for just a week, having been usurped by his rival and cousin Louis-Phillipe, Duc d'Orléans. He went into exile shortly after. Perhaps Henri's best legacy is having given his name to this rose. Unlike him, it is extremely robust and long-lasting.

Flower | Clear pink with lighter edges,
very double, 9cm (3½in) across
Habit | Upright shrub
Average height and spread | 1.5m x 1.2m (5 x 4ft)
Flowering | Repeat flowers
Scent | Strong and sweet
Aspect | Sunny
Type | Portland

MODERN ROSES

Starting with the hybrid teas, modern roses were developed, as their name suggests, with the modern gardener in mind. Rose breeders were, and most still are, in search of hardiness, practicality and easy of care, but also greater variety of colour and size, and – crucially – the ability to repeat-flower well.

English Roses

Since the 1960s English rose breeder David Austin has developed this wonderful new range of roses. His creations have the look and feel – and indeed the scent – of old roses but have the advantage of being repeat-flowering. They do well both in mixed borders and in rose gardens and come in a tempting range of colours and growth habits. Most are hardy and disease resistant. 'Gertrude Jekyll' (top left) is one of the most popular English roses, thanks to its vigour, striking double blooms and delicious fragrance.

Floribundas

First developed in the 1920s, floribundas are the result of crossing polyanthas with hybrid teas. Their name means 'many-flowered' and that's exactly what this perpetual-flowering group offers. The floribundas' beauty lies not in its individual blooms, nor in its scent (most have very little), but in its long-lasting clusters of flowers and disease resistance. Although many varieties display hot colours, the ever popular 'Iceberg' is a charming creamy white variety. Its vigorous climbing form (top right) can reach 4.5m (14¾ft).

Ground Cover Roses

Despite much variation in size, ground cover (or carpet) roses are generally wider than they are tall, thanks to long branches that grow horizontally. This spreading habit makes them great edging plants. They also look wonderful tumbling down steps, low walls and sloping banks. 'Laura Ashley' has small, pale magenta-pink flowers and tiny glossy leaves (bottom left).

Hybrid Musks

This group of strong, repeat-flowering shrub roses owes its existence to the Englishman the Rev. Joseph Pemberton, who started breeding them in the early twentieth century. Most have a delicious musk fragrance and double blooms borne in large clusters. Flowers come in a range of delicate hues, from creamy whites and buff yellows to pinks. Chief amongst the hybrid musks is the sweetly scented 'Buff Beauty' (bottom right) with its splendid peaches-and-cream blooms.

Hybrid Teas

Nowadays many of us love to hate hybrid teas, yet for many years they were the most popular roses around. Fans love their showy, continuously flowering blooms proudly carried on strong, upright stems. They are great as cut flowers and perhaps best grown in individual rose beds, being slightly too formal for the mixed border. Hybrid teas are

Top left *'Gertrude Jekyll', a much-loved English rose.* **Top right** *The climbing variety of 'Iceberg', which flowers abundantly throughout the season.* **Bottom right** *Flowers of the popular hybrid musk 'Buff Beauty' vary from rich apricot to shades of cream.* **Bottom left** *Ground cover rose 'Laura Ashley', with its small scarlet-mauve flowers and glossy leaves.*

a nineteenth-century introduction, the result of a crossing between a hybrid perpetual and a tea rose. The first of its kind was 'La France', introduced in 1867 by the French rosarian Jean-Baptiste André Guillot. 'Pot o' Gold' (top left) has lovely rounded fully double flowers – its rich gold colour is just one of the very many shades available from this class of rose.

Miniatures

The tiniest roses, miniatures grow to no more than 38cm (15in) tall and are characterised by thin stems and small blooms that repeat-flower profusely. Although often presented in nurseries and garden centres as indoor plants, they will not survive long inside. Nor are they ideal as container plants unless you are prepared to feed and water them regularly. Available in an astonishing array of colours and flower types, miniature roses probably all originate from *Rosa chinensis* 'Minima', a dwarf rose introduced from China in the nineteenth century. 'Mr Bluebird' (top right) has lavender-purple semi-double flowers held against dark green leaves; it reaches just 30cm (12in) making it perfect for the front of the border.

Patio Roses

Somewhere between a floribunda and a miniature, a patio rose is a compact cushion-forming shrub that produces clusters of flowers over a long season. As its name suggests it has been bred to grow in containers where it will thrive with just a little extra feeding, but it is equally happy in beds and borders. Much like miniatures, patio roses come in a huge range of flower shapes and colours. The sweet-smelling 'Sweet Dream' (bottom left) has beautifully formed peachy-pink blooms and grows to 43cm (17in) in both height and width.

Polyanthas

If you are looking for a small, floriferous and hardy rose, polyanthas are a very good choice. Developed in the late nineteenth century, these compact roses produce lovely sprays of small single or double flowers that bloom almost continuously. With its long-lasting, blossom-like blooms, 'Ballerina' (see page 44) is a popular choice. 'White Pet' (bottom right) is one of the most floriferous of all polyanthas: from June until the frosts it offers an endless show of white pompom-like rosettes. Despite its delicate looks, it is very tough and will handle almost any situation.

Ballerina

Its name may suggest graceful pink tutus but there is nothing dainty about this rose. It is one of the toughest you'll find.

It is also one of the most free-flowering. At its floriferous height, 'Ballerina' is covered in hundreds of tiny blossom-like flowers – so many that they almost hide the shrub's glossy foliage. From June onwards, single blooms appear in large hydrangea-like trusses, borne on the thinnest of stems. They come in varied shades of pink and white. The paler the flower, the older is it, petals gracefully bleaching with age and exposure to the sun. In the autumn, tiny hips offer an added beauty: flowers and fruit in the same season.

Apart from its hardiness and long flowering season, its key asset is an ability to combine with other plants, for this small and spreading shrub is one of the rose world's greatest minglers. It looks delightful in the classically romantic combination of pink roses, foxgloves, topiary balls and grey-leaved plants such as *Stachys* or *Lychnis*. For something a bit different, try mixing it with purples and deep crimsons, such as *Lupinus* 'Masterpiece', *Salvia nemorosa* 'Caradonna', *Penstemon* 'Raven' or *Knautia macedonica*. Mingled with such darker flowers, the light pink of its blooms really stands out. 'Ballerina' also works well as a low hedge, underplanted with lavender or catmint, while its hardiness makes it a popular choice as a standard in a rose garden or a more formal arrangement.

The naming of roses is full of alluring anecdotes and 'Ballerina' is a particularly sweet example. The story goes that its creator, the Rev. Joseph Pemberton, named it after his young great-niece, as she danced in his garden: an appropriate picture for such a joyful rose.

There is nothing quite as heart-warming as a rose flowering in the depths of winter. Whether you see it as symbol of hope in a bleak world or simply as a thing of beauty in unexpected surroundings, to witness the delicate blooms of 'Ballerina' clothed in a veil of hoar frost is one of winter's most uplifting sights.

Flower | Pale pink with white centre, single, 2.5cm (1in) across
Habit | Rounded, spreading shrub
Average height and spread | 1.2 x 1.2m (4 x 4ft)
Flowering | July to early winter
Scent | Slight musk
Aspect | Full sun, but tolerates some shade especially in hot climate
Type | Polyantha

CLIMBERS AND RAMBLERS

Both old and modern roses have climbing forms, whose stems grow to be much longer and more pliable than their bush-type relations. The variety of climbers and ramblers is vast. Generally, if you have a small garden, stick to small climbers. Ramblers need space to thrive and look their best.

Climbers

Often confused with ramblers, climbers are not as vigorous as their larger cousins, and their stems, though long and arching, are not as flexible. Their blooms, however, are bigger and often repeat-flowering, so there are advantages to growing this type of rose, particularly in the smaller garden. Deadheading will encourage a more generous second flowering while the horizontal tying of shoots will ensure more abundant flowers. Climbers are a varied bunch and exhibit a great many flower types and colours, so you are bound to find at least one to suit your plot. 'New Dawn'

(above) is one of the most reliable and healthy; it has semi-double, blush-pink flowers with a slight fruity scent and healthy foliage.

Ramblers

Tough yet elegant, ramblers are the graceful giants of the rose world. Their long stems are extremely pliable, making them easy to train up an arch, trellis or pergola. The most vigorous ramblers – known as scramblers – are best grown up large bushes, trees and buildings where they can reach well over 12m (almost 40ft) in height. All ramblers flower profusely in midsummer and most are wonderfully fragrant. For a few glorious weeks, they produce a stunning show of small to medium blooms, borne in abundant clusters that will cascade over arches, tumble down fences, and cover great swathes of wall. Considered one of the best and most beautiful ramblers, 'Paul's Himalayan Musk' (left) has dainty, deliciously scented, pale pink blooms.

PERFECT PARTNERS

For many gardeners the appeal of roses lies not just in their individual beauty, but in the many ways you can blend them with other plants. This approach has many advantages.

Dense planting suppresses weeds and ensures that the soil does not dry out and, if you plan your planting well, you can enjoy a long season of interest. A spring or autumn border can, for instance, be enlivened in midsummer with a few judiciously placed roses. Roses are some of the longest-flowering shrubs, and although June is their peak season, the repeat-flowering types will continue to bloom until at least late summer, making them an invaluable component in a coordinated planting scheme.

Planning a border from scratch can be daunting. Fortunately roses have the advantage of combining well with many other garden plants, and some make particularly good neighbours. In midsummer, campanulas (top left), delphiniums, foxgloves and hardy geraniums (top right) are some of the most valuable rose companions. Their blue and purple flowers harmonise well with the soft pinks and purples of old roses. They both enhance the allure of a rose and add dynamic interest to a composition. This is particularly true of foxgloves and delphiniums, and also of lupins (bottom) and verbascums, whose tall, stately spires are the perfect counterpoint to the rounded beauty

of a shrub rose. The purple, pink and white *Digitalis purpurea* 'Excelsior Group' is the classic choice of foxglove – a must for the cottage garden – but there are many other varieties in less common colours, such as butter-yellow and apricot-pink. Delphiniums also come in a range of tones, from white and blue to purple and even – though less successfully in my opinion – pink. Dark and blue lupins (such as 'Masterpiece' and 'Gallery Blue') look striking with maroon and pink roses, while pure white ones make great neighbours with creamy-yellow roses, particularly in yellow and blue themed borders.

Top left Rosa mundi, *underplanted with blue and white* Campanula persicifolia. **Top right** *Easy to grow and available in shades ranging from vivid magenta and deep blue to pale pink and white, hardy geraniums are an excellent partner for roses. Here Geranium psilostemon sets off a pale pink shrub rose.* **Bottom** *Purple and white lupins amongst the old roses at Sissinghurst Castle in Kent.*

Plants with small flowers, such as astrantias (left), linarias, nigellas and Russian sage, are useful for mingling through roses and creating a wispy effect. Such delicate and airy beauties soften a scheme and can help hold together different shades of rose. So too can grey and silver plants, including *Stachys*, *Lychnis* and *Artemisia*, which look especially beautiful in pastel arrangements of creams, blues and pale pinks.

Previous page *One of the best plants for adding vertical interest to the garden is the common foxglove, Digitalis purpurea. Being a biennial, it only flowers in its second year, so make sure you plant new foxgloves two years running to have blooms every summer.* **Left** *The sweet pincushion flowers of Astrantia 'Star of Royals' create the perfect framework around which to show off the small blooms of Rosa 'White Pet'.*

Fantin-Latour

Pale and interesting, this rose is so becoming you will want to grow it even though it flowers only once a year. Its pink blooms are light, but never so weak as to become pallid, and the flower shape is exquisite: a glorious frill of petals quartered around a charming button eye, beautifully offset by healthy, mid-green foliage. Centifolias are well known for their fragrance and 'Fantin-Latour' is no exception: its perfume is rich and sweet with strong citrus notes.

This arching shrub will grow to about 1.5m (5ft) tall and can also be trained as a climber up a wall where it will reach up to 3m (10ft). It blends well with silvery blues and purples, such as *Eryngium* and *Veronicastrum*, and looks lovely with a mass of ox-eye daisies, campanulas, lavender or *Linaria purpurea* at its feet.

French artist Henri Fantin-Latour was one of the nineteenth century's most celebrated flower painters. His pieces – quite a few of which feature old-fashioned roses in soft sorbet tones – have a wonderful spontaneity about them. He was able to capture the natural beauty of flowers without ever needing to embellish or perfect. Introduced in 1900, our mysterious rose is of unknown parentage and origin, but its name suits it perfectly, embodying as it does the pastel sweetness of Fantin-Latour's famous rose portraits.

Flower | Pale pink, double, 9cm (3½in) across
Habit | Arching, spreading shrub
Average height and spread | 1.5 x 1.2m (5 x 4ft)
Flowering | Summer only
Scent | Very fragrant and sweet
Aspect | Sunny
Type | Centifolia

Classic choices for underplanting roses are pinks, violets and the perennially popular *Alchemilla mollis*, (top left) attractive both for its scalloped, fresh green leaves and its froth of creamy yellow flowers. With its haze of lavender-blue flowers, catmint (top right) complements pink, white and pale yellow roses and is often used at the front of the rose border, where is does a great job of concealing a rose's least attractive feature: the leggy growth at its base. *Nepeta* 'Six Hills Giant', which grows up to 90cm (35 ½ in) in height, is best used with larger shrubs, while clump-forming dwarf catmints, such as *Nepeta × faassenii*, work well with smaller roses. Cut your catmint back after flowering and you will get another flush soon after.

Lavender (bottom left) is another good choice for the front of the rose border. As a young shrub it is much tidier than catmint, though more particular about its soil, which it prefers light and well-drained. Its scent, too, is a lot more attractive than that of catmint – to humans at least! *Lavandula angustifolia* 'Hidcote' is a popular variety: compact, it is both extremely floriferous and reliable.

If your rose is repeat-flowering, you could blend it with late-summer bloomers such as Japanese anemones and Michaelmas daisies. For a contemporary feel – stealing from the New Perennial approach – mix with grasses, salvias, persicarias, echinaceas and *Verbena bonariensis*.

If you have room in your garden for a show-stopping early summer border, one flower that teams up well with roses is the peony. Both are equals in the showiness stakes, but by interspersing them with more subtle blooms, their partnership can be superb. *Paeonia lactiflora* 'Sarah Bernhardt', with its double, soft pink flowers, is magnificent and the perfect match for an old or English rose. But others work well too, from the creamy white and double *P. lactiflora* 'Laura Dessert' to the opulent, coral-pink *P.* 'Coral Charm'.

Shrubs are easily overlooked but make valuable and versatile rose partners. Not only will they provide useful support for laxer rose species, but their contrasting flowers and leaves can create stunning combinations. Flowering shrubs such as *Philadelphus* and *Weigela* are natural partners for roses, as they flower in early summer, and their small blooms do not overpower the beauty of a rose. Shrubs with strongly coloured foliage, such as the purple-leaved *Berberis thunbergii* f. *atropurpurea*, are especially effective with purple and red roses. Shrubs that flower in late summer, such as buddlejas, will take off just after roses have peaked, creating a long sequence of blooms. And don't forget that larger shrubs make useful backdrops. The solid dark green of yew and box are classic choices as background hedges, setting off roses to full effect, while a bolder choice, such as the plum-coloured smoke bush, *Cotinus coggygria* 'Royal Purple' (bottom right), will provide a striking canvas against which to show off your rose. Another good variety is 'Grace', with larger foliage; if coppiced every year it makes a dramatic backdrop.

Top left *Alchemilla mollis looks particularly attractive with rich pink roses.* Top right *Catmints are a favourite partner for roses.* Bottom right *'Wild Eve' set off by the rich burgundy tones of* Cotinus coggygria *'Royal Purple'.* Bottom left *'Graham Thomas' underplanted with a haze of lavender.* Following page *Pale blue hardy geraniums and cerise-red* Paeonia lactiflora *'Felix Crousse' are among the many successful plant partners in the walled rose garden at Mottisfont in Hampshire.*

REACHING NEW HEIGHTS

Climbers, ramblers and standard roses add an extra dimension to the garden. And, as Gertrude Jekyll pointed out in Roses for English Gardens *(1902), growing a rose vertically means you can get up close to its flowers without having to stoop.*

'A perspective of rose pillars is a charming feature in a garden, and one of the ways in which their beauty may be best enjoyed,' Gertrude Jekyll wrote. 'They should be so placed that one can go right up to them and see the roses at eye level and below it and also against the sky, and smell their sweet scent in perfect comfort as they grow.'

A climber or rambler makes a beautiful backdrop to a border, but can work equally well on its own to clothe a wall, clamber up a trellis, arch or pergola, or scramble along swags. Jekyll has more useful advice when it comes to planting roses on pergolas. 'A rose pergola should be so placed that it is well seen from the sides. It ought to lead

Left *A climber graces the mellow stone walls at Great Chalfield Manor, Wiltshire.* **Right** *A simple garden bench at Compton Castle, Devon, is dramatically framed by the striking, deep-crimson climbing rose, 'Parkdirektor Riggers'.*

distinctly from some clear beginning to some definite end; it should be a distinct part of a scheme, otherwise it merely looks silly and out of place ... An arboured seat is always a good ending to a pergola.' Even for smaller features, such as a simple rose arch, it pays to think about your garden plan. Is there a natural spot that might lend itself to its placement, such as an entrance, the end of a path, or the point where two paths meet?

The choice of rose support will, of course, depend on your garden. In a rural spot, what could be more attractive than a jumble of climbing roses on a simple wooden picket fence? In a town or more formal garden, a metal arch or obelisk might be more appropriate. Even practical areas, such as the patio or vegetable garden, can be transformed into places of beauty and repose with a rustic rose arbour or pergola, creating useful shade and seclusion in the height of summer.

Left *The pergola at Polesden Lacey in Surrey is smothered in pink and white ramblers, including 'Dorothy Perkins' and 'Sander's White Rambler', shown here.*

Veilchenblau

Creating a truly blue rose has been the Holy Grail of rose breeders for centuries. Personally I find the idea distasteful, but I absolutely love *Rosa* 'Veilchenblau'. This sweetly scented beauty flirts with the idea of being blue, but always stays on the right side of purple.

Its semi-double, cup-shaped blooms emerge from their buds a rich magenta, then mature to a blue-purple before fading to a mauve-lilac. They have the added appeal of being flecked with white and having luscious yellow centres. Although it only flowers once, 'Veilchenblau' blooms generously for a good three to four weeks in high summer bearing large clusters of up to 30 small flowers. Autumn sees the tiniest reddish-brown hips gracing its almost thornless, pliable stems.

Trained against an old brick wall this rambler looks magnificent: the buff-toned canvas brings out the rich colouring of the flowers as well as the rose's light-green foliage. 'Veilchenblau' copes well with poor soils and cold temperatures and requires less sun than most roses, making it the perfect cloak for a north-facing wall. But it is equally happy growing up a rose arch, pergola or gazebo, or clambering up a tree or over a shed.

Like all ramblers it has a lively, organic feel about it, as if it could just carry on growing and growing, creeping over every surface it encounters, all the while sending up a tangle of stems with a fantastic froth of flowers. If you like the scent and spectacle of wisteria in May, you will adore this showy and richly fragranced rose.

Flower | Deep magenta or purple fading to blue-lilac, semi-double, 3.5cm (1¼in) across
Habit | Rambling
Average height and spread | 4.5 x 3.5m (14¾ x 11½ft)
Flowering | Once in midsummer
Scent | Sweet and fruity, reminiscent of lily of the valley
Aspect | Sun or part shade
Type | Rambler

Climbing and rambling roses make striking centrepieces on their own, but by associating them with other climbing and twining plants you can create even more pleasing combinations. Some of the best minglers are honeysuckles (top left and bottom left) – their small, delicate and usually heavily scented flowers will adorn a flush of roses like tiny lacy tiaras. The common honeysuckle, *Lonicera periclymenum*, works with almost any climbing or rambling rose, but there are lots of varieties to choose from. You could select one that displays a number of colours, such as *L. × heckrottii* 'Gold Flame' which has orange-yellow blooms flushed with pink, or you could go for striking orange (*L.* 'Mandarin'), creamy yellow (*L. periclymenum* 'Graham Thomas') or apricot-salmon (*L.* 'Celestial'). Whichever honeysuckle you choose, be sure to check if it has twining branches. Most do, but a few don't and these will need to be tied to a support.

Clematis (top right and bottom right) is the other great partner for roses. This is a hugely varied group, with a flowering range that extends from early spring to autumn, and a wonderful choice of gorgeous colours displayed on single, double or trumpet-shaped flowers of different sizes. Of the early flowering varieties the single-flowered and fast-growing *C. montana*, which comes in shades of pink and white, needs a large space and therefore makes a great duo with any of the rambling roses.

Combining a small-flowered rose with a large-flowered clematis, or vice versa, works well, as neither type of bloom competes with the other. It is almost impossible not to create attractive colour harmonies with these two plants. Clematis in shades of purple ('Étoile Violette', 'Jackmanii'), blue ('Prince Charles' or 'Perle d'Azur') and pink ('Comtesse de Bouchaud' or the small, trumpet-flowered 'Princess Diana') look particularly romantic with pale pink and yellow roses, but more striking combinations look equally glorious.

One of the joys of gardening is that you can experiment in your own plot and roses are the ideal plant with which to do so. As garden writer and rose enthusiast Patrick Taylor once wrote: 'There are some plants that bring out the best in roses. But roses are not fastidious about the company they keep. One of their greatest charms is that they will bring out the best in an immense number of other garden plants.'

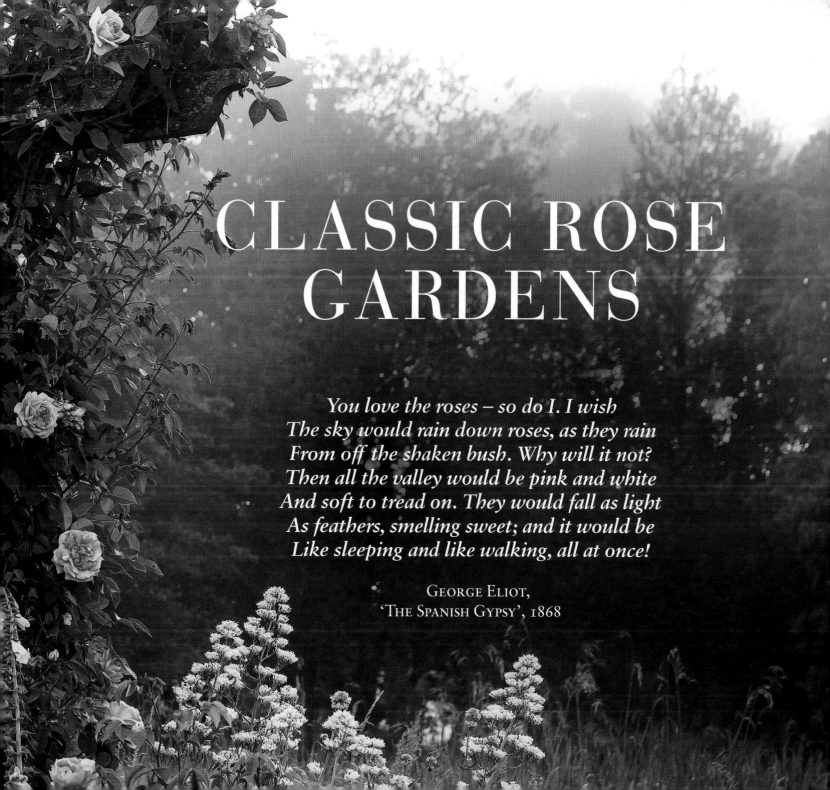

CLASSIC ROSE GARDENS

You love the roses – so do I. I wish
The sky would rain down roses, as they rain
From off the shaken bush. Why will it not?
Then all the valley would be pink and white
And soft to tread on. They would fall as light
As feathers, smelling sweet; and it would be
Like sleeping and like walking, all at once!

GEORGE ELIOT,
'THE SPANISH GYPSY', 1868

BATEMAN'S
East Sussex

Rudyard Kipling, owner of Bateman's, wrote the much-lauded poem 'The Glory of the Garden', in which he celebrates the joys of gardening.

There is no doubt that Kipling loved his own garden at Bateman's. A setting for family gatherings and a much-needed retreat, he designed many of its elements. From the scented rose walk to the climbers and ramblers gracing the garden's many walls, Kipling's love of roses is everywhere evident. But it is especially so in the Rose Garden, which he designed himself – together with the adjoining Lily Pond – using the prize money he was awarded for winning the Nobel Prize for Literature in 1907. Recently restored, the Rose Garden features two of the floribundas – *Rosa* 'Betty Prior' and 'Frensham' – planted by Kipling, and a new addition, 'Valentine Heart'. It is a simple yet beguiling arrangement in shades of pink and scarlet.

Left *Designed in the early twentieth century by Rudyard Kipling, the formal Rose Garden at Bateman's features the floribundas 'Betty Prior' (mid-pink), 'Frensham' (red) and 'Valentine Heart' (pale pink).*

Cornelia

There is so much to recommend 'Cornelia' that it is difficult to know where to start. Its colour is irresistible: the blooms are a luscious candyfloss pink dotted with warm apricot centres. The sweet coral-tinted buds have a particular charm too – they look like little carnations. Combine these winning features with pretty ruffled petals, a sweet scent, fine dark-green foliage and maroon-coloured stems and you have a superb-looking rose. But 'Cornelia' isn't just attractive. It is healthy and repeat-flowering and tolerates more shade and rain than most roses – and it makes a great cut flower.

This is quite a large, spreading shrub, with flowers appearing in large clusters, and does well in the mixed border. It works both with warm colour schemes of reds and purples, and with blues and yellows. Thanks to its peach-coloured centres, it harmonises beautifully with apricot-yellow roses, such as *Rosa* 'Buff Beauty' – another hybrid musk of great charm.

Because it flowers for such a long period, make sure you consider late summer pairings. For restrained elegance go for the pure white charms of *Anemone × hybrida* 'Honorine Jobert'. For something a little more relaxed, opt for a hazy mass of tall lavender-blue Michaelmas daisies, such as *Aster × frikartii* 'Mönch', underplanted with sedums. If you are restricted for space, 'Cornelia' can be grown on its own up a low trellis or metal obelisk, where it will create a romantic centrepiece.

Flower | Light strawberry pink with apricot centres, double, 5cm (2in) across
Habit | Vigorous shrub
Average height and spread | 1.5 x 1.5m (5 x 5ft)
Flowering | Repeat flowers
Scent | Strong and sweet
Aspect | Sun or partial shade
Type | Hybrid musk

BORDE HILL GARDEN
West Sussex

With 17 acres (7ha) of formal gardens, each with its own feel, Borde Hill is one of the great Sussex gardens.

Although perhaps most famous for its collections of rare trees and shrubs, particularly magnolias, camellias, rhododendrons and azaleas, one of Borde Hill's other highlights is Jay Robin's Rose Garden, designed in 1996 by RHS gold medallist Robin Williams. Here you will find over 100 varieties of David Austin roses planted in formal beds and culminating in a charming circular pool. Swathes of lavender and catmint add haziness to the design which, together with delphiniums and peonies, harmonise with the soft-pink roses.

Right *Borders are edged with neat box hedging and punctuated by decorative obelisks.*

This page *An elegant fountain proudly stands at the centre of the formal Rose Garden at Borde Hill.*

BROUGHTON CASTLE
Oxfordshire

A romantically moated manor house within acres of parkland is the wonderful setting for this beautifully designed and lovingly tended garden, where roses take centre stage.

Roses fill the long, deep borders in this immaculately designed and maintained garden, whose jewel in the crown is the walled Ladies' Garden. You will want to linger in this secluded spot, where shrub roses in shades of pink and cream steal the show. Blended with delphiniums, foxgloves, nepeta and alliums, they create a pleasingly frothy effect. It all seems effortless, yet it is planned and maintained to perfection. While you are visiting the house, make sure you look down at the Ladies' Garden from above. From this vantage point the fleur-de-lis patterns of the central beds become obvious and remind us that gardens are not just meant to be walked through.

Left *Rosa 'Gertrude Jekyll', Astilbe chinensis 'Vision in White' and a deep blue delphinium make a powerful trio in one of the exquisite borders at Broughton Castle.* **Right** *A soothing mix of whites, blues and greys with a sprinkling of yellow, the border at the entrance to the Ladies' Garden is composed of roses, delphiniums, day lilies and lambs' ears (Stachys byzantina).*

Left *This tightly packed border in a corner of the Ladies' Garden brims with roses, nepetas, delphiniums, alliums and evening primroses (Oenothera biennis).*

CLIVEDEN
Buckinghamshire

Cliveden is famous for its Italianate mansion designed by Charles Barry, but it is also home to some exceptional gardens, of which its Rose Garden is a small but exquisite gem.

The Rose Garden was designed in the late 1950s by the architect and garden designer Sir Geoffrey Jellicoe for the then owner of Cliveden, William Waldorf Astor II. It was a small, secluded garden intended as a retreat from Lord Astor's busy life as a businessman and politician. Sadly, over the years the roses succumbed to disease and by the early 2000s the garden was no longer thriving. Its re-creation, instigated in 2013, is a triumph. Here you will find over 800 repeat-flowering roses, ranging from pale yellow to bright orange and intense red dotted with colour-coordinated arches and benches and a few classical statues. Unlike many other rose gardens which rely on old roses, this one blooms from mid-June right through to September.

Right *Named after the celebrated piece of music by Vaughan Williams, 'The Lark Ascending' is a charming English rose with pink-apricot tones.* **Far right** *A bright mass of Rosa 'Fellowship' graces the foreground while 'Warm Welcome' flowers on the arch.*

Right *The Rose Garden at Cliveden has been carefully designed as a great sweep of colour ranging from yellow through to red. Here, apricot-yellow Rosa 'Lady of Shalott' blends with sunset-pink 'Summer Song', which in its turn merges with crimson-red 'Thomas à Becket'.*

COUGHTON COURT
Warwickshire

Not many people know this but the rose garden at Coughton Court is one of the finest in the world. In 2006 it received the Award of Garden Excellence from the World Federation of Rose Societies – the only British garden ever to have been granted this accolade.

Although it covers a fairly small plot, what the rose garden lacks in size, it more than makes up for in floral punch and masterful planting. Over 200 varieties of rose flourish here, amongst hundreds of herbaceous perennials and a few carefully dotted annuals. At first the effect is overwhelming – there is so much to take in – but this is exactly what its creator Christina Williams intended. She did, after all, call it the Rose Labyrinth. You need to get lost in it: that is the point. And the more you do, the more you will enjoy it.

An award-winning garden designer, Christina made the rose garden in 1996 as a gift for her mother, Clare McLaren-Throckmorton, who – until she sadly passed away in 2017 – owned the estate at Coughton Court. Although the National Trust has been in charge of the Tudor mansion since 1946, the 25-acre (10ha) grounds are still managed by the Throckmorton family. When Lady Throckmorton inherited the estate in 1993, she decided to create a series of new gardens to set off her ancestral home. Over the last 25 years they have matured beautifully and now offer a delicious mix of enclosed, designed garden 'rooms' and wilder open spaces. Visitors can enjoy exquisite long borders, a formal courtyard garden, sunken gardens, riverside walks, a bog garden, a bluebell wood, and attractive fruit and vegetable gardens. But the Rose Labyrinth – bedecked with so many gems in June and July – is Coughton's summer centrepiece.

'I didn't want to have an old-fashioned mono-culture of roses,' explains Christina. 'I wanted to grow all sorts of roses: climbers, ramblers, old-fashioned shrub roses, some good teas and floribundas, modern shrubs and new English roses. Some I just wanted for their names: 'William Shakespeare', 'Ispahan', 'Gertrude Jekyll', 'Abraham Darby' …' Covering a roughly rectangular plot, in what used to be the old vegetable garden, Christina's creation relies on a series of archways with small, serpentine paths that take you past an incredible concentration of plants planned in separate yet seemingly connected beds – all of which 'allow the visitor to get lost in a maze of colour and scent'.

At the centre of the garden is a statue of Rosamund Clifford, mistress of Henry II and kinswoman of the Throckmorton family. Known as 'Fair Rosamund', she was one of the great beauties of her age; her charms have inspired many ballads, poems and paintings, including a few by the Pre-Raphaelites. To conceal the affair from his wife, Eleanor of Aquitaine, Henry hid Rosamund in a maze in the grounds of his palace at Woodstock, Oxfordshire, but clever Eleanor found her way through the intricate network and poisoned her rival.

Rosa mundi

Rosa mundi is the irresistible sweetie in the candy shop that is the rose world. Its swirling, bi-coloured petals produce a scrumptious raspberry-ripple effect of pale pink striped and flecked with crimson. And, as Vita Sackville-West remarked, no two petals are the same: 'Sometimes they come in red orderly stripes, sometimes in splashes, sometimes in mere stains and splotches, but always various, decorative, and interesting.'

Officially known as *Rosa gallica* 'Versicolor', *Rosa mundi* is a cultivar of the wild gallica rose and one of the oldest cultivars of any plant grown today. Legend suggests it was named after the twelfth-century 'Fair Rosamund', mistress of Henry II. This is an appealingly romantic story, but experts now believe it to be false, and so its origins remain a seductive mystery.

This vigorous low-growing shrub produces a mass of large blooms with a spicy scent. Although it flowers only once, it does so for a long time. Because of its variegated flowers, it usually works best in simple colour arrangements. For a fresh effect, pair it with *Alchemilla mollis*, whose soft green leaves complement the rose's own foliage and help bring out the vibrancy of its blooms. Astrantias (try *Astrantia* 'Roma' or *A.* 'Buckland') make a particularly exquisite partner. Their delicate, star-shaped flowers do not overpower our rose; instead they dot the arrangement with attractive, lace-like umbels.

Rosa mundi looks great with other old roses – pastel pink and crimson would be my choice – mixed with box topiary and maybe a few ferns and the tall spires of pale cream *Verbascum* (try *V.* 'Spica'). Like all gallicas, it has a tendency to sucker and so works well as a low hedge. At Greys Court in Oxfordshire, it edges both sides of the path in the orchard and in high summer creates the most striking – and deliciously scented – foreground to the long grass and apple trees beyond.

Flower | Pink striped with crimson, semi-double, up to 10cm (4in) across
Habit | Bushy, upright shrub
Average height and spread | 1.2m x 1.2m (4 x 4ft)
Flowering | Once in summer
Scent | Warm musk
Aspect | Sunny
Type | Gallica

Young and demure looking, Coughton's Rosamund holds a single rose in one hand and is surrounded by beds of her namesake rose, *Rosa mundi*. Unbeknownst to you, she is your destination, though you will pass many other (horticultural) beauties along the way. A few carefully placed benches encourage you to take your time and savour the journey.

While the family remains very much at the helm, Jamie Vickers, who has been working at Coughton for over ten years and was appointed Head Gardener two years ago, cares for the gardens with the utmost attention to detail. 'I've learnt everything on the job,' he says modestly, though his additional RHS training and David Austin rose pruning courses have stood him in good stead. 'We didn't use to prune the roses hard enough. They had become leggy and weren't blooming as much as they could.' Everything, not just the pruning, is carefully considered. 'We try to keep as much space as possible around the base of most roses so that they get the nutrients they need – but you won't notice any bare soil in the summer. And we lift and divide almost all perennials annually.' Work carries on once the garden goes to sleep, when the bulk of the pruning takes place. In all it can take about six to eight weeks to get done. Jamie's thorough approach has paid off. The garden is resplendent and the plants show no signs of disease.

Madame Isaac Péreire

This wonderful rose is generous in every respect: its scent is one of strongest you are likely to encounter; its cupped flowers are huge and of the richest magenta-pink; even the plump buds are full of promise and they certainly deliver. 'Madame Isaac Péreire' blooms lavishly into the autumn, when it produces its best flowers. No wonder demand for this beautiful Bourbon rose has not waned since its introduction in 1881.

Both intense and delicious, the intoxicating fragrance has been compared to the smell of ripe fruit, particularly raspberries. The flowers are equally pleasing: elegantly quartered with ample petals turning back on themselves at the ends and brilliantly offset by deep green foliage.

Because of its long stems and open habit, this large shrub is often grown as a climber or pillar rose. Train it up an arch or pergola – somewhere you are likely to walk past or sit beside – so you can savour its perfume often. It also makes a great focal point at the back of the border and, although it goes particularly well with other deep or blush-pinks, purples and lavender-blues, I find that pale peach and apricot-coloured roses, such as David Austin's 'Crown Princess Margareta', make exquisite pairings.

'Madame Isaac Péreire' was developed in France by a humble gardener named Armand Garçon. He christened his creation 'Le Bienheureux de La Salle' ('Blessed la Salle') after Jean-Baptiste de la Salle, founder of a religious institution where Garçon may have been taught as a young boy. Garçon then sold his rose to breeders Margottin Père & Fils, who renamed it after the wife of the wealthy Parisian financier, Isaac Péreire, and promptly took the credit for the rose. Garçon was subsequently re-ascribed his creation, but his original name has yet to be used.

Flower | Purple-crimson, double, 12cm (4¾in) across
Habit | Tall, open and arching shrub
Average height and spread | 2.5 x 2.1m (8¼ x 7ft)
Flowering | Repeats in flushes
Scent | Rich and sweet
Aspect | Sunny
Type | Bourbon

Roses are trained and pruned in a variety of ways depending on their habit. *Rosa glauca*, for instance, is left pretty much to itself, allowing its stems to bend gracefully and its flowers to bear hips. Archways play host to grape vines, clematis and, of course, lots of climbing and rambling roses. Amongst these are 'Bleu Magenta' with its small violet-crimson blooms; the yellow to milky-white 'Goldfinch'; and 'Alchymist', whose superbly scented double flowers range from golden-yellow to deep orange.

A few standard roses add height and variety amongst the borders, while some of the shrub roses have been trained to create, as at Sissinghurst (see pages 144–165), great mounds of flowers. Each of these has been planted around a metal pole from which 8–12 wires branch out. 'We let the rose grow freely for about two years then we tie all the top growth to the wires. You don't want to leave this too late, as the stems get too woody and will not bend as much.' Despite all the hard graft, Jamie's bond with the place is clear to see and he gets much pleasure and solace from his work. In times of stress, he turns to his favourite rose, *Rosa* 'Gertrude Jekyll'. One sniff and his calm is restored.

Left *Snaking pathways lead you past billowing borders and rose-heavy arches.* **Top right** *Floriferous and strongly fragranced, Rosa 'Fantin Latour' forms a shapely, healthy shrub.* **Far right** *'Little White Pet' is prized for its bright white blooms and healthy, glossy foliage.* **Bottom right** *English rose 'The Pilgrim' has beautiful, fully double, soft-yellow blooms.*

Rosa glauca

Rosa glauca is an exceptional rose. Although fleeting, its flowers – the simplest of blooms – are enough to recommend it, but its unique foliage and plentiful crop of hips are what make it really worthwhile. Few roses are so versatile or have such a long season of interest.

The mass of small, blue-grey leaves of this graceful, arching shrub creates the perfect foil not only for its own flowers, but for other plants too. Remarkably, the leaves appear to change with the weather. In full sun they look almost coppery purple; in the shade they light up to a lovely slate grey. Flowers are followed in late summer by bountiful scarlet hips that last until winter.

Hardy and easy to grow, *Rosa glauca* has a refined wildness that makes it ideal for more naturalistic plantings and cottage gardens. It is a great choice for hot colour schemes of reds and purples – berberis, continus and *Clematis viticella* are great allies – but it harmonises well with most colours. It looks exquisite with low-growing grey plants such as sedums and lambs' ears (*Stachys byzantina*), but is equally alluring in a woodland-inspired, green-and-white scheme of ferns, cow parsley and bluebells. For a contemporary effect, plant it with large grasses such as *Cortaderia richardii*.

Rosa glauca is not a showy rose – perhaps the ultimate antidote to hybrid teas, all flower and nothing else. It wears its beauty lightly, but once experienced, you're unlikely to forget it.

Flower | Crimson pink fading to mid pink,
single, 2cm (¾in) across
Habit | Vigorous, arching shrub
Average height and spread | 2.1 x 1.8m
(7 x 6ft)
Flowering | Summer only
Scent | Insignificant
Aspect | Sun and part shade
Type | Species rose

Left *Shrub roses harmonise with allium seedheads, white foxgloves,* Stachys byzantina *and* Alchemilla mollis *against the copper beech* (Fagus sylvatica purpurea) *backdrop.* **Right** *White rosebay willowherb* (Chamaenerion angustifolium *'Album')* and Rosa *'William Lobb' form a dazzling duo.*

Combine such dedication and hard work with intricate, artful planting and you have a winning combination. Every twist brings a new arrangement of roses and perennials, where colour and shape have been carefully orchestrated. Some areas are quieter than others. Soft pink roses such as *Rosa* 'Comte de Chambord' harmonise with pale blue hardy geraniums or purple nepetas, and lime-green *Alchemilla mollis*. Other corners offer bolder groupings of deep pinks (*Rosa* 'Madame Isaac Péreire') and bright blue delphiniums, softened with salmon-pink achilleas and a haze of bronze fennel. Plants with silver leaves are a particular favourite of Christina's, including *Santolina pinnata* subsp. *neapolitana* 'Edward Bowles', *Artemisia ludoviciana* 'Valerie Finnis', and *Stachys byzantina*, which spills onto the paths along with heucheras, violets and other low-growing perennials.

Tall airy plants such as *Verbena bonariensis*, bronze and green fennel and the red *Scabiosa atropurpurea* set off the roses without ever stealing the limelight. As Christina explains, 'Roses *en masse* can appear a bit blobby,' so her design relies on plenty of spire-shaped plants, as well as ones with strappy leaves. There are lots of pink and white foxgloves and vibrant delphiniums, but also salvias and a dreamy mass of white rosebay willowherb (*Chamaenerion angustifolium* 'Album'), which forms a delicate backdrop to the heavenly scented *Rosa* 'Gertrude Jekyll' and the velvety, purple-magenta moss rose 'William Lobb' (above). Other staples include irises, alliums, peonies, penstemons, the steely grey-blue thistle *Eryngium bourgatii* and the upright-stemmed, butter-yellow *Sisyrinchium striatum*. 'It self-seeds everywhere,' says Jamie, 'but works really well with the roses.'

Two sides of the rose garden are edged with copper beech, a striking backdrop against which to show off the colourful planting. A high wall of ancient red brick supports climbers and ramblers, while the fourth side of the garden opens onto pillars of roses with meadows and the River Arrow beyond. From this vantage point, you get a glimpse of the rest of the garden, where you will find other lovingly tended roses, not least in the immaculate Courtyard Garden, whose formal beds are crammed full of wonderfully healthy looking *Rosa* 'White Pet' (see page 97).

Having made your way around the entire garden, past immaculate borders and sharp lawns, avenues of pleached branches and bountiful fruit and vegetable gardens, you may well be tempted to wander back into the Rose Labyrinth. Here maybe, just maybe, you will find your way not to Fair Rosamund, but to the equally seductive *Rosa* 'Gertrude Jekyll', to draw in her sweet, comforting scent.

Left *The main path in the rose garden, edged with long double borders. On the left is a beautiful pairing of the pure pink Rosa 'Gertrude Jekyll' and the taller, purple-magenta moss rose 'William Lobb'.*

Nevada

'Nevada' is the queen of white roses. In full bloom, this large shrub is smothered in a profusion of huge, single to semi-double saucer-shaped flowers. They're so copious that they overlap, as if jostling for attention. The whole thing is a spectacular sight, but as they vie for your gaze it pays to look closely at individual flowers.

Despite its name meaning 'snow-covered' in Spanish, 'Nevada' doesn't actually have snow-white blooms. They are in fact ivory white, tending towards cream, and have the most luscious honey-coloured centres topped with a crown of yellow stamens. 'Nevada' flowers early, often in late May, in a great flourish. This is followed by intermittent blooming, and then another show in late summer, when the flowers are sometimes tinged with pink, making it look almost like a different rose.

But where to plant such a large shrub? How about at the end of the garden, where the planting is often freer? On its own it grows into a great mound with arching stems – the perfect backdrop against which to place smaller flowers and shrubs. If your garden is large enough, mix it with other shrubs. Blending it with another rose is not a bad idea and you could do worse than to grow it with its pink sport, *Rosa* 'Marguerite Hilling'. It is basically the same rose, but with pink blooms.

'Nevada' was created by the Spanish rosarian Pedro Dot in 1927. His other great creation is the much-loved pink-flowered 'Madame Grégoire Staechelin'. Like 'Nevada', it has huge flowers and blooms early. It is one of the most spectacular early-flowering climbers and one of the most reliable.

Flower | Creamy white, semi-double,
12.7cm (5in) across
Habit | Large, spreading shrub
Average height and spread | 3 x 4m (10 x 13ft)
Flowering | Early, once fully, then intermittently
Scent | Very light
Aspect | Sunny
Type | Modern shrub rose

DAVID AUSTIN ROSES
Shropshire

This is the glorious home of the English rose, where you can enjoy discovering hundreds of these wonderful flowers in beautifully designed and inspiring settings.

David Austin Roses is not just one of the top rose nurseries in the country, it is also a series of attractive rose gardens showcasing over 700 varieties of our favourite flower, enhanced by sculptures and architectural features. At its centre lies the Long Garden, home to an outstanding collection of old roses. The Victorian Walled Garden is predominantly planted with English roses, enhanced with climbers and ramblers on arches, arbours and walls. The Renaissance Garden is all about English roses, while the Lion Garden's long borders feature pleasing combinations of shrub roses and herbaceous perennials. A must for anyone who loves old and English roses.

Right *A display of shrub and climbing roses in the Lion Garden.* **Far right** *Created by David Austin in 2006, Rosa 'Lady of Megginch' has large, cupped blooms displaying a rich, deep pink.*

Right *The Long Garden, with its rose-covered pergolas and plentiful borders.*

Constance Spry

When David Austin created *Rosa* 'Constance Spry' in 1961, he unwittingly made rose history. This was his first commercially available rose and the beginning of a long line of brilliant creations, each taking as their inspiration the character, fragrance and romantic appeal of old roses. 'Constance Spry' effectively paved the way for his ever-popular family of English roses.

Unlike most David Austin roses, 'Constance Spry' only flowers once, but what a show it provides! Its blooms – large and abundant – are the clearest, purest of pinks. Its silky petals curve gently inwards, making the flower's centre alluringly elusive, while its rich myrrh fragrance bewitches passers-by.

It is a tall shrub, with long and unruly branches that need plenty of support and so is best grown up a trellis, pergola, arch, wall or wooden fence, where it looks fabulous on its own or interlaced with other climbing roses (such as the creamy white rambler, *Rosa* 'Albéric Barbier') or clematis. Ideal border companions are ferns, hardy geraniums (try the magenta *G.* 'Patricia' for vibrancy), campanulas, lavender, nepeta, aconites and, most sentimental of all, delphiniums (pastel blue ones, such as *D.* 'Emily Hawkins', are my favourite).

Fittingly, this epoch-making rose is named after the founder of modern flower arranging. Constance Spry, who adored old roses, cultivated many antique varieties at her school of cookery at Winkfield Place in Berkshire and was instrumental in their revival. She became popular for her striking compositions, gaining commissions from the well-to-do and the royal family – famously doing the flowers at Princess Elizabeth's wedding in 1947 and her coronation in 1953. It would have pleased her to know that her own rose makes a very good cut flower.

Flower | Pure pink, double and cupped, 10cm (4in) across
Habit | Strong, arching shrub
Average height and spread | 1.8 x 1.8m (6 x 6ft)
Flowering | Once in midsummer
Scent | Spicy and rich
Aspect | Sunny
Type | English rose

HELMINGHAM HALL
Suffolk

Helmingham Hall is home to the award-winning garden designer
Xa Tollemache. Her much-admired, meticulously maintained
garden bears the mark of her outstanding skill.

Within the grounds of this double-moated Tudor mansion are glorious herbaceous borders, dreamy wildflower meadows, an enchanting potager and immaculate knot and herb gardens. In 1982 Xa Tollemache added the Rose Garden: beds of damasks, Bourbons, moss and China roses, as well as modern hybrid perpetuals and English roses, mingle with herbaceous plants, while standard roses and taller shrub roses add depth and rhythm to this pleasing, pastel-coloured composition. Elsewhere in the grounds you will find roses aplenty: a parterre edged with hybrid musks, climbing roses scrambling over red-brick Tudor walls, arches draped in pale pink *Rosa* 'Debutante', and more.

HEVER CASTLE AND GARDENS

Kent

William Waldorf Astor spared no expense when he created his magnificent formal garden in the early years of the twentieth century.

Over 1,000 men were employed to shape and plant the landscape at Hever, helped by steam engines and horses to shift rocks, soil and mature trees. There is much to enjoy here, including a superb Italian Garden filled with Astor's collection of classical statuary. The exquisite Rose Garden, boasting over 4,000 bushes ranging from albas and Bourbons to hybrid teas and floribundas, is formal in style and planted in coloured blocks. Since 2011, the garden has its very own rose: the velvety *Rosa* 'Hever Castle' (Horquinsey), which produces masses of deep red flowers against glossy, dark green foliage from June through to September.

Left *Each flower of the virtually thorn-free English rose 'Geoff Hamilton' forms a perfect cupped rosette, almost peony-like in shape.* **Right** *The Rose Garden at Hever Castle is planted in colour-themed beds and dotted with classical features.*

Left *The Italian Garden at Hever Castle with its profusion of abundantly flowering roses.*

KIFTSGATE COURT

Gloucestershire

A short walk from Hidcote, Kiftsgate is as memorable as its more famous neighbour.

The setting of Kiftsgate Court, on the edge of a Cotswold escarpment, is magnificent and the planting luxuriant, organised in a series of enclosures and borders, many of which feature shrub roses. In the double Rose Border, old species and modern roses mix freely, with one side almost taken over by the huge and spectacular, *Rosa filipes* 'Kiftsgate'. It grows almost unchecked, reaching through the tallest trees and creating cascades of small pure-white flowers in early to mid-July. Look out for another single-bloomed white beauty: *Rosa sericea* 'Heather Muir', named after the first of three generations of gifted women who have gardened here.

Right *The path in the Rose Border Garden at Kiftsgate Court is edged with plantings of the bi-colour Rosa mundi, a few of which have reverted to their one-toned parent rose, Rosa gallica var. officinalis.*

MOTTISFONT
Hampshire

Every rose enthusiast should make the pilgrimage to Mottisfont at least once in their lifetime. Hiding behind weathered red-brick walls is one of the most enchanting rose gardens you are ever likely to encounter.

During a few weeks in midsummer, hundreds of climbing and shrub roses show off their charms in fragrant clouds of white, pink and crimson. If gardens are all about scent, spectacle and escape, then Mottisfont is the queen of them all.

It is a heady, otherworldly space, especially come evening when the scent of so many roses, trapped all day within four walls, becomes almost intoxicating. A sensual alchemy is at play, mingling fresh citrus bouquets with rich, spicy aromas. Evocative names summon visions of yesteryear: *Rosa* 'Great Maiden's Blush' and *Rosa* 'Belle Sans Flatterie' bring to mind young ladies of bygone days, 'Souvenir de la Malmaison' harks back to Empress Joséphine's great rose garden near Paris, and 'Ispahan' conjures the exotic delights of Ancient Persia.

Everywhere the focus is on old roses, for Mottisfont holds the National Collection of Pre-1900 Shrub Roses. Albas, damasks, gallicas, Bourbons and Chinas, they are all here. Once-flowering, often heavily scented and double-flowered, these are lavish, generous gems. Within these walls are over 500 different varieties of rose, many of which originate from the collection of just one man: the great rosarian Graham Stuart Thomas (1909–2003). It is him we must thank for saving old roses from near extinction in the second half of the twentieth century.

Despite this hugely important legacy, Mottisfont is much more than a rare botanical survival. It is a work of art. As John Sales, Head of Gardens at the National Trust between 1971 and 1998, succinctly put it, Mottisfont is 'Graham's masterpiece'. Graham Stuart Thomas is best remembered as a passionate and influential rose collector, but he was also a plantsman and nurseryman, a skilled garden designer and gifted artist, photographer and writer.

Thomas was born into a family of keen amateur gardeners from Cambridge and by the age of eight had already decided he was going to pursue a career in horticulture. A turning point in his life was no doubt the year 1931, when he made the acquaintance of Gertrude Jekyll. At the time Thomas was working as a foreman at Hillings Nursery near Chobham in Surrey and Jekyll lived nearby at Munstead Wood. They became friends, enjoying discussions about plants and garden design, Jekyll sharing with the young Thomas her thoughts on colour theories and instilling in him her credo of gardening as art. It was at this time that Thomas began to collect old roses.

Graham Thomas

This is the most popular of all yellow roses, and deservedly so. 'Graham Thomas' will reward you with a continuous show of richly scented flowers from the start of summer through to the first frosts.

Borne in clusters, its cupped golden blooms fade to a light apricot as they age. There are no harsh lemon yellows here, just deliciously soft shades, set against perfect mid-green leaves. No wonder 'Graham Thomas' was once voted the World's Favourite Rose by members of the world's 39 National Roses Societies.

This is a tall shrub, so make sure you have room for it, or opt for its climbing version, which harmonises beautifully with honeysuckles and blue clematis, such as C. 'Perle d'Azur' or the darker 'Wisley'. As a shrub 'Graham Thomas' works well with the blue and purple hues of salvias, campanulas, nepetas and delphiniums, but it is also beautiful with yellows, whites (white foxgloves look exquisite) and pale greens. Here the colour of its blooms can really be appreciated.

Lovers of old roses should grow 'Graham Thomas' for no other reason than to celebrate its namesake – for this was the man who almost single-handedly revived the fashion of old roses in the last quarter of the twentieth century. From the tender age of 15, Graham Stuart Thomas became obsessed with roses. He went on to develop one of the world's greatest collection of old roses, which he subsequently donated to Mottisfont Abbey in Hampshire (see page 122). He wrote copiously on his subject, resolute – and indeed absolutely right – in the belief that 'people instinctively love gardens designed for roses'.

Without Graham Stuart Thomas would his friend David Austin have ever developed his own English roses, inspired by the charms of old roses? Possibly not. So it is only right and proper that David Austin should have created this particular rose, first introduced at the Chelsea Flower Show in 1983, in honour of the master rosarian.

Flower | Golden, double, 10cm (4in) across
Habit | Upright, vigorous shrub
Average height and spread | 1.5 x 1.5m (5 x 5ft)
Flowering | Repeats well
Scent | Strong and fruity
Aspect | Sunny
Type | English rose

His first publication on roses was a booklet entitled *The Manual of Shrub Roses*. In its foreword he makes clear his aim 'to bring forth these lovely things from retirement'. This was followed by three books – *The Old Shrub Roses* (1955), *Shrub Roses of Today* (1962) and *Climbing Roses Old and New* (1965) – which arguably did more to spread the word for old-fashioned roses than anything else.

Working as Gardens Adviser for the National Trust between 1955 and 1974, Thomas was responsible for restoring and reviving over 100 gardens throughout England, Wales and Northern Ireland. This was a time of unprecedented activity in heritage gardens, when such now-famous sites as Hidcote, Sissinghurst, Stourhead and Powis were acquired by the Trust and thoughtfully restored for the general public to enjoy. Thomas was at the helm of these exciting developments. He was, as John Sales writes, 'a unique phenomenon,' who 'pursued his own vision of perfection relentlessly, even ruthlessly, in every aspect of his life.' It is a life that deserves closer study.

Thomas's sharp artistic sense, his immense knowledge of plants and his two decades at the Trust culminated in the creation of the aesthetically refined garden at Mottisfont. His collection of roses, assembled over many years, finally found the home it deserved when the old vegetable garden at Mottisfont became available in 1971.

Left *Lavender edges the wall-bound border, densely packed with old roses in charming shades of pink.*

As Thomas later recalled, the event 'coincided with a desire of the National Trust to establish a collection of old shrub roses ... Practically all the old European roses still in cultivation are there – gallicas, damasks, centifolias, mosses ... Together with old ramblers and climbers on walls and pillars there is at Mottisfont a fairly complete picture of the roses grown up to about 1900, with the emphasis on the ancestral species and their early derivatives ... The rose's pomp will be displayed far into the future at Mottisfont, where my work of some thirty years collecting these varieties together from France, Germany and the US, and numerous gardens and nurseries in the British Isles, will not be set at naught.'

From the start, Thomas was aware of the original walled garden's advantages, writing in his 1991 book on Mottisfont, *An English Rose Garden*: 'Few better sites could have been found for a garden of old roses than this.' The soil was rich and fertile having been well dug and manured over the years. Ever respectful of the past, Thomas worked with the traditional layout of the old kitchen garden, retaining its paths, box hedges and central dipping pool – a fitting framework within which to place a series of rose borders, deftly underplanted and interspersed with a mix of herbaceous perennials and annuals. He also retained several of the garden's old apple trees, 'which made good hosts for climbers.'

Left *Rosa 'Indigo', a deep pink, highly fragrant Portland rose, stands out against a backdrop of fairy bellflowers (Campanula persicifolia).*

Madame Hardy

This ravishing damask rose is like the most exquisite wedding dress. Its delicate fabric is tailored to perfection: nothing is out of place, everything dainty and immaculate.

Long leafy sepals envelop pale pink buds that slowly unfurl to pure white, beautifully formed petite flowers with ruffled petals and a light-green button eye. Blooms appear only once, but for a long period, and give off the slightest of sweet scents against a backdrop of fresh, mid-green leaves. The effect is exquisite and 'Madame Hardy' certainly deserves its reputation as one of the most outstanding of all white roses.

Despite its tender appearance, this is a strong bushy shrub with lots of healthy foliage, very good disease resistance and an ability to thrive in semi-shaded areas. It looks gorgeous on its own or grown with other old roses. My choice would be old light pink varieties – nothing should compete with the pure white of Madame Hardy's blooms. Why not try other damasks such as the clear pink and strongly scented 'Ispahan' or the full-petalled, slightly darker 'Marie-Louise'?

Also known as 'Felicité Hardy', 'Madame Hardy' was named after the wife of its creator, Julien-Alexandre Hardy, chief gardener at the famous Jardin du Luxembourg in Paris between 1817 and 1859. As well as being a tree expert, he has been credited with developing over 200 roses; 'Madame Hardy', introduced in 1832, is without doubt his most famous.

Flower | Pure white, double, 6cm (2½in) across
Habit | Tall, upright shrub
Average height and spread | 1.5 x 1.5m (5 x 5ft)
Flowering | Once in midsummer
Scent | Slight but delicious and sweet
Aspect | Sun or part shade
Type | Damask

A gateway set in a sunny, rose-covered wall leads to the first and largest of two rose gardens. Along the walls are long gravel walks with box-lined beds filled with shrub roses and topped with ramblers, climbers and clematis. Either side of the central path are two deep borders planted with Thomas' favourite perennials selected to complement his shrub roses. This companion planting is varied but relies on many traditional and much-loved staples, such as foxgloves, delphiniums, campanulas and penstemons. Paths are edged with pinks, while jumbles of purple and pink linaria and wispy love-in-a-mist (*Nigella damascena*) bring softness to the planting. Elsewhere, accents and contrasts are created by spiky-leaved, electric blue irises. Grey tones – so flattering to roses – come in the form of sages, artemisias and ever-so-tactile lambs' ears (*Stachys byzantina*).

Follow the main path and you will reach a central pool and fountain guarded by eight clipped Irish yews. Here, Thomas writes, 'the severity of the hedges and topiary are contrasted by the elegant lines of the garden seats, metal copies of an eighteenth-century design. All these lines and that of the coping round the pool are firm and formal. In contrast are Nature's flowing lines and informal exuberance of rose "Raubritter" – in full sun, billowing over the side of the pool at the centre of the rose garden … It is the only rose I know which could be controlled to the shape that I needed for this position.' This short extract demonstrates Thomas' thoughtful approach to design. It also neatly summarises one of his guiding principles – an idea inspired by the Arts and Crafts approach to gardening – of strong formal bones contrasted with exuberant and loose planting. Other structural elements come in the form of a long wooden pergola and arches dripping with climbers and ramblers.

Above *The sweet, candy-coloured blooms of Rosa 'Debutante', a charming rambler.* **Right** *Wormwood, Lychnis coronaria 'Alba' and Linaria purpurea 'Canon Went' frame the silvery pink blooms of Rosa 'Felicia'.*

The second rose garden is a smaller, more intimate space, which Thomas deliberately planted in a slightly cooler colour palette. As he recalls in *An English Rose Garden*, 'My colleagues and I were desirous that this new garden should be quite different from the first, and have a fresh impact. This was all the more important because the main ingredients were to be similar.' The paths here are wider and follow the line of the walls round a roughly triangular plot. The central feature is, as described by Thomas, 'a brick-paved circle, with a series of stout, chamfered oak posts connected by iron hoops – which we call a bower, as in Victorian days.' The latter is clothed in free-flowering *Rosa* 'Bleu Magenta' and clear pink 'Debutante' and underplanted with 'Comte de Chambord' (see pages 38–39). Paths are edged with lavender instead of box, a softer alternative which works well with the lighter shades of this garden, as do the grey-leaved, white rose campion (*Lychnis coronaria* 'Alba') and pale purple alliums.

As with all great gardens, Mottisfont exudes artistry, attention to detail and, above all, a love of plants. In *The Art of Planting* (1984) Thomas wrote: 'Whether you look upon gardening as a hobby, a science or an art, the fundamental point returns again and again: that we garden because of the beauty of plants.' How right he was.

PECKOVER
Cambridgeshire

Peckover House lies at the heart of one of Britain's most beautiful Georgian streets. Few of the visitors who come to marvel at Wisbech's North Brink are aware that behind these distinguished buildings is a garden of equal refinement.

While Peckover House is pure Georgian, its garden is mostly Victorian. There are exotic specimens gathered from plant-hunting expeditions, greenhouses bursting with blooms, and carpet bedding in all its vibrant efflorescence. Roses take centre stage in Alexa's Rose Garden. This peaceful spot was re-created in 1999 using old photographs showing rose arches surrounding a small lily pond. Climbing roses such as the small cream and pink *Rosa* 'Phyllis Bide', candy pink 'Madame Grégoire Staechelin', and crimson-flecked 'Honorine de Brabant' are a romantic sight in late June and early July, when walls, pillars and arches throughout the garden are heavy with clusters of roses, just in time for Wisbech's long-established Rose Fair.

Left *Rosa 'Sander's White Rambler' scrambles over the arch in Alexa's Rose Garden.* Right *A simple arch, clothed in Rosa 'Hiawatha', marks the end of a gravel path edged with double borders designed by rosarian Graham Stuart Thomas.*

QUEEN MARY'S GARDEN

Regent's Park, London

A brilliant, manicured show of over 12,000 roses in 85 single-variety beds, Queen Mary's Garden is by far London's largest and most impressive rose garden.

In midsummer, the scent and spectacle of the roses in Queen Mary's Garden are overwhelming. When it was created for Mary, wife of King George V, in 1932 the garden focused on hybrid teas and floribundas. Renewed in the 1990s, it now has examples of most rose varieties, each clearly labelled. The showpiece is a central fountain surrounded by swags draped with climbing roses. Other great London rose gardens worth visiting can be enjoyed at Hyde Park, Kew Gardens, Hampton Court Palace and Holland Park.

Left *These glorious swags are the perfect host for the vigorous rambler 'Seagull'.* **Right** *The pretty rambler 'Evangeline' produces sprays of pale pink flowers later in the season.*

Left *This border at Queen Mary's Rose Garden is filled with varieties of David Austin-created English roses.*

RHS ROSEMOOR

Devon

Rosemoor might be one of the RHS's regional gardens, but it is of national importance and second only to RHS Wisley.

Rosemoor's 65 acres (26.3ha) contain over 3,500 plants from across the world, showcased in a variety of spaces. You will find cottage, foliage, bog and winter gardens, endless herbaceous borders, model gardens, colour-themed gardens, and two delightful spots that focus purely on roses. The formal Queen Mother's Rose Garden boasts over 60 varieties of hybrid teas and floribundas, fancifully arranged in a colour wheel, from white and pink shades to red, orange and yellow. The Shrub Rose Garden, meanwhile, blends over 120 types of old roses.

Right *Prized for its dark green, glossy foliage and lily-white flowers, Rosa 'Sander's White Rambler' is one of the most popular ramblers. Here it is on the pergola in the Queen Mother's Rose Garden at RHS Rosemoor.*

SISSINGHURST CASTLE GARDEN

Kent

When Vita Sackville-West and her husband Harold Nicolson acquired Sissinghurst in 1930, there was very little to recommend it. The place was a jumble of ruined buildings, worthless junk and rampant weeds.

Despite first appearances, in Sissinghurst Vita had found her paradise. 'I fell in love at first sight. I saw what might be made of it. It was Sleeping Beauty's Garden.' She and Harold would reawaken it.

As they started work in the garden, clearing the weeds in the orchard, they came across an old rose (which was later named 'Sissinghurst Castle'). It was the only flower in their new plot, but what a flower! With its dark purple, velvety blooms and its mysterious origins, this was just the kind of plant that spoke to Vita's love of romance and history.

Right *Rosa californica 'Plena', a semi-double species rose with hollyhock-shaped lilac-pink blooms.* **Far right** *One of the paths in the Rose Garden, where borders brim with the most romantic arrangements of roses and perennials.*

Since this prescient moment, roses have become the brightest stars of Sissinghurst. They are everywhere: simple yet elegant species roses; ramblers and climbers covering ancient walls; and fountains of richly scented shrub roses. No wonder Vita once declared herself 'drunk on roses'. Like Graham Stuart Thomas, she had a passion for old roses. She loved their histories and evocative names, their fragrance and delicate beauty. And they suited her generous planting style – as she said, 'my liking for gardens to be lavish is an inherent part of my philosophy.'

Despite being a novelist, columnist, diarist, poet and biographer, Vita Sackville-West (1892–1962) is best remembered today for the garden she created at Sissinghurst and for her tumultuous affairs with women, most famously Virginia Woolf. During her lifetime, her novels, including the still-popular and highly recommended *All Passion Spent* (1931), enjoyed much success and, although she failed to reach the status she desired as a poet, her epic poem *The Land* (1926) is still regarded today as a lyrical celebration of the English countryside. Vita was also a great populariser of gardening. She opened Sissinghurst to the public in 1938 and between 1946 and 1961 wrote weekly columns for *The Observer*, which she cynically referred to as her 'sticklebacks'. 'Even the smallest garden can be prodigal within its own limitations,' was one of her mantras.

Left The Rose Garden at Sissinghurst, a magical mix of scented roses and herbaceous perennials, at its glorious height in late June. Right Sweet williams (Dianthus barbatus), delphiniums and foxgloves are some of the many traditional companion plants in the Rose Garden.

Complicata

Don't be fooled by its name: there is nothing complicated about this rose. Its flowers are some of the simplest and loveliest in the rose world and it is very easy to grow.

Happily, it is also one of the first roses to bloom. 'Early in the season they are the most spectacular roses to be found,' wrote rosarian Graham Stuart Thomas. The flourish of candy-pink flowers with their white centres and honey-hued stamens is a cheering sight in early summer.

Although it has the look and feel of a wild rose, *Rosa* 'Complicata' is thought to be a cross between the French gallica rose (*Rosa gallica*) and the dog rose (*Rosa canina*) – hence why it is sometimes referred to as a 'glorified dog rose'. Like its parents it only flowers once, but don't let that put you off. Apart from a lavish summer flowering, you will be rewarded with a great crop of red hips in the autumn.

This is a vigorous shrub that can become very large so give it plenty of space, and the long arching branches can do with some support. It looks glorious growing up a pillar or, even better, a tree, as can be seen at Mottisfont in Hampshire (see page 122), where it clambers up one of the walled garden's old apple trees. For a cottage-garden effect, underplant it with easy-going perennials such as *Alchemilla mollis* or blue geraniums (*Geranium* × *johnsonii* 'Johnson's Blue' has particularly attractive deep lavender flowers), and maybe a sprinkling of alliums.

Unlike many roses, 'Complicata' tolerates shade and so is also ideal for the woodland garden or the orchard, where it can reach its full height and spread.

Flower | Rose pink with a pale centre, single, cupped, 12cm (4¾in) across
Habit | Large, arching and spreading shrub
Average height and spread | 2.4 x 1.5m (7¾ x 5ft)
Flowering | Once in June
Scent | Light and sweet
Aspect | Full sun or part shade
Type | Gallica

Vita's greatest sorrow was the loss of Knole, her beloved ancestral home in Sevenoaks, which she failed to inherit because she was a woman. Her childhood was shaped by this gigantic Elizabethan mansion, with its hundreds of rooms and thick layers of history. It was her playground and her domain – fertile ground for a young, imaginative mind. Sissinghurst, which also dates from Tudor times and was once owned by a Sackville, was Vita's attempt to re-create something of Knole's atmosphere and restore that connection to her past which she so missed. And, like Knole, it was place in which one could hide: a refuge composed of what Harold called 'a series of privacies'.

Sissinghurst is indeed a garden of rooms, whose strong bones are softened by abundant planting. Harold was the architect, drawing up plans to make sense of an irregular site dotted with old buildings and walls. He was the classicist, Vita the romantic, but their talents merged (not without the odd disagreement!) to create a dynamic and alluring work of art.

As soon as they moved to Sissinghurst, Vita and Harold started making their new home habitable. The tower came first – this is where Vita would write in glorious isolation. The South Cottage would house Harold's study and a couple of bedrooms. On 6 May 1930 the couple planted their very first rose against its front wall: the early flowering *Rosa* 'Madame Alfred Carrière' (left) – jokingly referred to as 'Mrs Alfonso's Career' by Harold – which is still going strong today. The Priest's House (far left) would have bedrooms for their sons, Ben and Nigel, and a family dining room. The old stables were to be converted into a library-cum-sitting room. Everyone had his or her space, but the garden was their constant and common backdrop. It was the glue that held the buildings, and the family, together. You had to walk through it to get anywhere.

Left *Looking towards the Priest's House, situated on the edge of the gardens.* **Above** *'Madame Alfred Carrière' creeps happily up the ancient walls of the South Cottage. It has a wonderfully fruity fragrance.*

Sissinghurst Castle

We have Vita Sackville-West to thank for the revival of this sumptuous rose. Not long after she and her husband Harold Nicolson acquired Sissinghurst Castle in 1930, they discovered an old gallica rose growing amongst the tangled weeds of their new garden.

No one is quite sure of its origins – although it is also known as 'Rose des Maures' – but Vita nurtured it back to glorious life and it became commercially available, under its new name, in 1947. You can still buy 'Sissinghurst Castle' from a handful of specialist nurseries. It is worth searching out, and not just for its superior provenance. This neat upright shrub has gorgeous velvety flowers and does exceptionally well in poor soils and in pots.

Flecked with the slightest hint of white and veined with darker streaks of purple, the rich crimson petals crease and curve around warm gold stamens, often revealing only part of the flower's heart. A tantalising sight, and one which surely pleased Vita very much.

She adored roses; they are the stars of her garden. In its heyday, she and Harold grew over 200 different roses at Sissinghurst. Vita loved old-fashioned shrub roses the best – the more romantic the better. She relished their sensuous beauty, their 'generosity' as she called it, and their evocative names and heritage. How wonderful then that there is a rose named after one of the most famous rose gardens in the world, and that we can grow a piece of Sissinghurst in our own plot.

Flower | Magenta-crimson, semi-double, 7cm (2¾in) across
Habit | Upright shrub
Average height and spread | 1 x 1m (3¼ x 3¼ft)
Flowering | Once in midsummer
Scent | Light
Aspect | Sunny
Type | Gallica

It is worth starting your visit by climbing the tower and viewing the garden from above. Here you realise just how good a designer Harold was. He imposed logic and structure where there was none. Long axes, such as the Yew Walk, are bisected by shorter straight paths; there appear to be square and rectangular spaces, and a circular area, known as the Rondel, surrounded by yet more yew hedging.

From the outset, the couple wanted a garden of seasonal features. This still holds true today. In April, the Lime Walk is a carpet of scillas, grape hyacinths, narcissi and the snake's head fritillaries. The famous White Garden peaks in early summer, but many of the garden rooms look good throughout the growing season. The Cottage Garden, although reaching a zenith of hot colours in late summer, puts on a show from May onwards, when tulips, wallflowers and opium poppies burst into flower. The Orchard, a haze of blossom and narcissi in April, turns into a wild rose garden come June when the apple trees are smothered in rambling sprays of species roses.

At this time of year, roses are a constant in most parts of the garden, from the very moment you enter it. *Rosa* 'Meg' welcomes you in, its large apricot-pink blooms like proud sentinels on the warm, red-brick walls. In newly planted beds below, scented hybrid musks 'Pink Prosperity', 'Penelope', 'Cornelia' and 'Felicia' enhance the floral spectacle.

William Lobb

This splendid, vigorous rose has exotic airs that are hard to resist. Its large blooms are the texture of sumptuous velvet with ruffled petals of the most intense purple-pink, turning a powdery lavender with age. Thickly mossed stems and buds add to the rose's peculiar charm and its heady aroma is intoxicating.

'William Lobb' is justly considered one of the best moss roses. Vigorous and disease-resistant, it deserves a prominent place in the garden, where for a few weeks in summer it will steal the show. Due to its large size and generous flowering, it benefits from some support and sits best at the back of the border, where it looks exquisite with other purples, as well as blues, pinks, lilacs, fresh greens and greys.

Attractive partners include indigo-blue *Salvia* × *sylvestris* 'Mainacht', thistle-like *Cirsium heterophyllum*, wildlife-friendly *Hesperis matronalis* and dark-stemmed *Penstemon* 'Dark Towers'. More traditional choices are the ever-popular *Nepeta* 'Six Hills Giant', fresh-green and versatile *Alchemilla mollis*, as well as a whole host of easy-to-grow hardy geraniums, in shades ranging from the lightest blue to the richest magenta.

French rose-breeder Jean Laffay introduced 'William Lobb' in 1855. He named it after the famous Cornish gardener and plant-hunter now best remembered for the commercial introduction into England of the monkey puzzle tree (*Araucaria araucana*). William Lobb began a craze that would see a strange-looking conifer become the icon of the Victorian garden. The monkey puzzle is a striking addition to any plot, much like his namesake rose.

Flower | Deep purple-pink, double, 9cm (3½in) across
Habit | Vigorous shrub, can also be trained as a climber
Average height and spread | 2.5 x 1.5m (8¼ x 5ft)
Flowering | Once in midsummer
Scent | Strong
Aspect | Sun or partial shade
Type | Moss

This page *Alliums, foxgloves, potentillas and irises: just a few of the plants adding to the rose displays in the Rose Garden.*

These recent additions are part of a drive from Head Gardener Troy Scott Smith, who came to Sissinghurst in 2013, to increase the number of roses in the garden. Scouring Vita and Harold's notebooks and diaries, he and his team discovered that the couple had almost 200 different old roses at Sissinghurst. They realised that only about 100 were still growing in the garden and so, since 2014, have been planting them back, filling gaps and following Vita's maxim to 'cram, cram, cram, every chink and cranny'. The planting is wonderfully rich and lavish and displays an artistry of design for which Troy Smith is renowned.

As you go through the first archway and enter the Front Courtyard you realise just how central roses are to Sissinghurst. Here more walls drip with, in Vita's words, 'a tumble of roses'. Amongst the climbers is *Rosa* 'Mermaid', a primrose-yellow single rose dating back to Vita and Harold's time. One of the many showstoppers on the opposite wall is the frothy pink rambler 'May Queen' pruned in a typically loose fashion. Vita hated over-pruning, describing the rose 'as a wildly blossoming shrub'. In the ample borders below are showpiece species roses *Rosa moyesii* and *Rosa moyesii* 'Geranium', their crimson blooms and long arching stems adding vibrancy, grace and height to the displays (left and right). Vita loved dark purple, velvety roses such as *Rosa* 'Charles de Mills', 'Tuscany Superb' and 'Cardinal de Richelieu' and the south-facing Purple Border is a celebration of plants displaying these rich tones.

Left *With large, vibrant-red flowers, Rosa moyesii 'Geranium' is one of the most striking of all species roses.* **Right** *The same rose in the autumn. Its orange hips look particularly attractive amongst these greens and purples.*

This colourful outburst is calmed right down in the famous White Garden. Here you will find the huge rambler *Rosa mulliganii* (shown left and right), which smothers a large metal arbour in small, musk-fragranced flowers, creating a huge frothy cloud of scented trusses. But look closer and you will find more discreet yet equally beguiling treasures amongst the lilies, lupins, delphiniums and willowherb: early flowering *Rosa spinosissima*, the sumptuous 'Madame Hardy' with its green button eye, camellia-like *Rosa* 'Boule de Neige' and the exquisite 'Blanchefleur', whose lightly blushed blooms emit a rich, sweet scent.

Vita was a fan of 'wild gardener' William Robinson, who advocated a more natural approach to gardening. Like Gertrude Jekyll, he wanted to see roses clambering up trees and growing in meadows. Vita saw the Orchard as an opportunity to experiment with this freer style. Today this wildly romantic spot is dotted with a variety of species roses: they climb up trunks and poles, clamber through the old apple trees and scramble amongst the grass. But it is in the Rose Garden that roses reach their peak of lushness and abundance. Amongst the foxgloves, alliums, irises, peonies and other herbaceous perennials, roses steal the show.

Here, in what was a kitchen garden until 1937, they thrive in the heavy Wealden soil, enriched by years of generous feeding. The hundreds of shrub roses are shown off in a variety of ways. One particular approach, pioneered by Vita's Head Gardener Jack Vass, consists of gently bending rose stems into arcs and tying them to wires to form hoops. This technique encourages more flowers, creating wonderfully dense mounds of blooms. Some of the less rampant rose species, such as *Rosa glauca*, are left to grow in their natural, unaltered state. Dotted around are roses growing up poles, acting as exclamation marks in the borders.

Left *Sissinghurst's most famous highlight, the White Garden, in its midsummer haze.* **Above** *The huge rambler* Rosa mulliganii *comes into flower slightly later than other roses, producing huge trusses of white blooms.*

It is in the Rose Garden that you can really appreciate Vita's love of old roses. There are gallicas, damasks, centifolias, Bourbons and mosses aplenty – too many to mention but all, as Vita poetically put it, 'more romantic the one than the other'. From the clear pink, fresh beauty of *Rosa* 'Complicata' and the striped raspberry-ripple blooms of *Rosa* 'Camaieux', to the dark, mossy delights of 'William Lobb' and the deep crimson, heavily scented 'Zigeunerknabe', you will want to take your time to appreciate the individual qualities of these blooms. As Vita once wrote, 'a collection of old roses gives a great and increasing pleasure'. If only she could see how much delight her flowers continue to give.

Rambling Rector

What a giant of a rambler this is! Magnificent in full bloom, it will scramble up the tallest trees, walls and buildings and colonise the wildest corners of the garden, offering great clouds of deliciously scented blooms in midsummer.

Clusters of tiny semi-double flowers begin life a delicious buttercream with golden centres, turning bright white with age while the stamens get darker. Abundant flowering gives way to masses of small orange hips that look particularly attractive against the turning autumn foliage.

'Rambling Rector' is often hailed as the perfect cloak for hiding unsightly features in the garden – old sheds, crumbling walls, large tree stumps, unshapely or dying trees. This it does with relish – so much so that trees will actually look as if they are flowering – but it can also be grown on its own, when it will develop into a huge foamy mound.

Its flexible branches mean you can train it along a pergola in a genteel manner reminiscent of the best Edwardian gardens. As with most climbing plants, horizontal and angled stems flower more abundantly than vertical ones, so stretching the branches sideways will produce more blooms. Unlike most roses, 'Rambling Rector' is happy in the shade and therefore ideal for covering a large, north-facing surface.

For a more controllable rambler, you can cut it right back, but it takes a lot of work to keep this beast under control. Best to let it go wild (although annual pruning is required) and enjoy waves of frothy flowers, year after year. You'll never want to go on holiday in June again.

Flower | Creamy white fading to pure white, semi-double, 4cm (1½in) across
Habit | Vigorous rambler
Average height and spread | 6 x 4m (19½ x 13ft)
Flowering | Once in midsummer
Scent | Strong musk
Aspect | Sun or shade
Type | Rambler

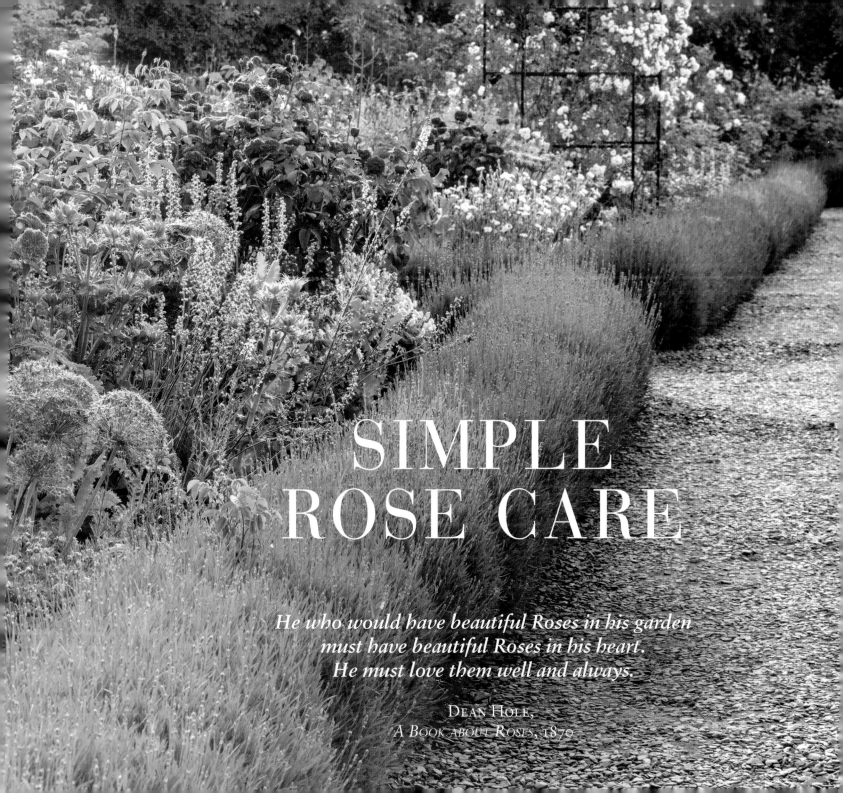

SIMPLE ROSE CARE

He who would have beautiful Roses in his garden
must have beautiful Roses in his heart.
He must love them well and always.

DEAN HOLE,
A BOOK ABOUT ROSES, 1870

Roses are easy to grow and, once established, do not require too much attention. Follow these simple instructions and your roses will flourish, giving you radiant blooms, healthy leaves and cheerful hips year after year.

PREPARING THE SOIL

Roses will grow in almost any reasonably well-drained and fertile soil. What roses don't like is having wet feet or being overly dry. If your soil is heavy clay, dig a deep hole where you are planning to plant your rose, add some gravel to the bottom and refill with the original soil mixed with manure, compost and grit. On dry sandy soils, which don't retain nutrients, add plenty of garden compost and well-rotted manure (preferably in winter).

CHOOSING THE RIGHT PLANT

Always buy a rose from a reputable nursery, garden centre or rose grower. Bare-root roses – by far the best option – come in a greater variety than containerised ones and can be ordered online or by mail order. Your rose will be delivered between late autumn and late winter when it is in its dormant state. This is the best time for planting as it helps the rose develop a strong root system. If you buy a pot-grown rose – available from garden centres all year round – make sure it has established good roots within its pot, or wait until it has done so before planting it. (You can check this by slowly lifting the plant out of its pot: if it comes out as a whole and the roots are showing on the outside, then they have had time to bind with the soil and you can plant your rose.)

PLANTING

Dig a hole about 50cm (almost 20in) deep and wide, add lots of well-rotted manure, fork it in and – if possible – leave the soil to settle for a few weeks. With bare-root roses, soak the roots in a bucket of water about an hour prior to planting. Select the best four or five stems and prune back quite hard to about four buds from the base. Remove the remaining stems completely, including anything damaged, crowded or crossing ones. This may seem quite harsh but will repay you with a much stronger and better-shaped plant in the long run.

Do not try to plant your rose if the soil is frozen. You can leave it in its packaging for about a week, where its roots should remain moist. If the bad weather continues beyond this point, take the rose out of its wrapping and place it in a bucket or a large pot filled with damp compost until the weather improves.

Your planting hole should be wide enough for the roots to be spread out – 50cm (almost 20in) should be big enough. The graft union of your rose should be about 2.5cm (1in) below soil level. Once you have placed your rose in the planting hole, sprinkle it with a mycorrhizal fungi (available from garden centres and from specialist rose growers). This will greatly improve the vigour of your rose, encourage its establishment and help suppress any soil-borne diseases.

Next, holding your rose with one hand, slowly add the prepared soil back into the hole, regularly firming it down with your heel as you go. It is important you do this as there should be no air pockets next to the roots. Finally, add a thick mulch of manure.

When planting a pot-grown rose, remove it from its container and place it in the planting hole, following the instructions above. Do not be tempted to tease out the roots (like you would when planting herbaceous perennials and other plants), as this can cause damage to the delicate root system.

PRUNING

Many people worry about pruning, but it is actually quite simple. There are just a few basic rules. The aim is to create an open-centred plant, free from damaged, diseased or too many crossing stems. The idea is also to stimulate the right sort of growth for flowering shoots. As a rule, the nearer a rose is to a wild species type, the less pruning it will need. Prune once a year and always use clean, sharp secateurs. For all roses first remove any dead, damaged or diseased wood and crossing stems. All cuts should be no more than 5mm (⅕in) above an outward-facing bud: this will encourage an open shape and help avoid crossing stems. Always make a sloping cut away from the bud; this will ensure that rainwater flows away from it and therefore stop it from rotting.

Species and Old-fashioned Shrub Roses

These roses flower once a year in midsummer on shoots produced from older wood. They require only light pruning to keep the centre of the plant open and free from excessive crossing stems. Reduce young, soft side shoots by about one-third if necessary and occasionally completely remove very old main stems to the ground, favouring a younger stem to take its place. This can all be done in late summer, once flowering is over.

Left *Make sure you gather up your cuttings; never leave them under the plant. Burning diseased leaves and stems will help prevent the spread of further illness.*

Repeat-flowering Shrub, Modern and Bush Roses

These roses flower more than once through the year, usually on younger wood. They perform best with slightly harder pruning done when the rose is dormant, between December and late March. Follow the principles of keeping an open-centred bush but pruning the whole thing a bit harder and a bit lower. On modern bush roses such as hybrid teas, cut each main stem down to about seven or eight buds from the base.

Ramblers

Once the plant is at its fully established height, remove one-third of the oldest stems annually in late summer. Tie in younger stems as replacements then shorten back all side shoots by two thirds.

Climbers

In winter, cut the flowered side shoots back to about three buds from the main stem. On older plants remove one or two of the oldest stems right to the ground and tie in a younger stem as a replacement.

A healthy rose is quite tough and forgiving and you would have to work very hard indeed to ruin a healthy rose through pruning! Keep to these basic principles and you can't go wrong. Once you are confident you can experiment with different types of training on pillars or supports – the final look of your rose garden is largely dependent on how you prune your roses. For the relaxed old-fashioned look prune lightly; for a more formal manicured look prune harder.

DEADHEADING

This involves removing faded or dead flowers after they have bloomed. Regular deadheading encourages more flowers to be produced. Gently snap off the faded flower with your finger and thumb. Remember to leave the deadheads on species roses if you want to see the hips!

WEEDING

The roots of roses are very close to the surface of the soil, so careful hand weeding is recommended. Once you have removed all the weeds, gently loosen the soil around the rose and apply a generous mulch of well-rotted manure. Spring weeding should be followed by a feed, as per the following instructions.

FEEDING

In spring, after you have weeded the ground around your rose, apply a general-purpose or rose fertiliser, following the instructions on the packet. Then top with a thick layer of well-rotted manure or compost, making sure the mulch does not touch the rose stem; a 10cm (4in) gap is ideal. During the flowering season, roses in containers need twice-monthly feeds with a liquid fertiliser.

PESTS AND DISEASES

The best way to avoid any problems with roses is to look after them well by pruning, weeding, mulching and feeding them as instructed above. But some pests and diseases are hard to avoid altogether. Thankfully, there are simple techniques to help you tackle some of these common rose problems.

Aphids

These small sap-sucking insects, also known as greenfly and blackfly, are active in spring and summer and appear on rose buds, shoots and young leaves. They produce sticky honeydew that can cause mould and distort flower buds. Be on the lookout for aphids in spring when your rose starts producing new growth. You can reduce their numbers by simply picking them off by hand, or you can try to spray them off with a water hose (but make sure you don't damage the delicate rose buds). Organic sprays can also help, but be diligent and do not be afraid to reapply if necessary. Ladybirds love feasting on aphids, so it's worth encouraging them in your garden by growing pollen-rich flowers and herbs, such as marigolds, chives, dill, fennel, yarrow, cosmos and scented geraniums.

Black Spot

This fungal infection is the most common of all rose diseases. As its name suggests, it manifests itself by black or dark brown spots on leaves. The stems may also have dark blotches. If left untreated, leaves eventually wither and fall off the plant, leaving your rose considerably weakened. As soon as a new infection occurs, remove all affected leaves and stems and rake away any fallen leaves from under the plant. Do not put them on the compost heap, as this may cause the fungus to spread. Next, spray your rose with an organic fungicide and repeat the treatment after two weeks.

You can help prevent black spot by following these simple steps. Water your rose in the morning. This will allow the water to evaporate from the leaves during the day and discourage the black spot fungus, which thrives in damp, warm conditions. Make sure your rose is open and there are no crossing stems: this promotes healthy air circulation.

In the autumn or early winter remove all fallen leaves from under your rose. Mulch it generously with a good layer of well-rotted manure before the spring.

Powdery Mildew

Another fungal disease, powdery mildew causes a white powder on leaves, stems and buds. The leaves turn grey or brown and fall off, and the buds never have a chance to fully open. Powdery mildew is more likely to affect climbers and ramblers and roses grown in a sheltered situation with poor air circulation. It is often the result of high humidity combined with dry soil and poor airflow. You can help prevent the disease by mulching and feeding your rose well and watering it generously during dry spells. When powdery mildew strikes, cut back all affected leaves and shoots, clear away any leaves at the bottom of the plant and water thoroughly. Spray with fungicide during the growing season and in late summer/autumn to help prevent the fungus from overwintering on the rose.

Rust

Less common than black spot and powdery mildew, rust is another fungal disease that appears in spring and summer. Look out for yellow spots on top of the leaves and dusty orange ones underneath. This is followed by black or dark brown pustules in late summer and leaf drop soon after. As with powdery mildew, prune all infected leaves and stems and destroy them. To prevent rust, make sure your rose has plenty of room around it so that air can circulate. Happily, many new rose varieties are rust resistant.

FURTHER READING

Austin, David, *David Austin's English Roses*, Conran, 1993

Austin, David, *The Rose*, Garden Art Press, 2013

Beales, Peter, *A Passion for Roses*, Mitchell Beazley, 2004

Beales, Peter, *Classic Roses*, Harvill Press, 1997

Eastoe, Jane, *Vintage Roses: Beautiful Varieties for Home and Garden*, Pavilion, 2016

Jekyll, Gertrude and Mawley, Edward, *Roses for English Gardens*, 1902

Nicolson, Adam, *Sissinghurst Castle Garden*, National Trust, 2018

Potter, Jennifer, *The Rose*, Atlantic Books, 2010

Quest-Ritson, Charles and Brigid, *RHS Encyclopedia of Roses*, 2008

Raven, Sarah, *Vita Sackville-West's Sissinghurst: The Creation of a Garden*, Virago, 2014

Robinson, William, *The English Flower Garden*, Cambridge University Press, 2011

Sackville-West, Vita, *Some Flowers*, National Trust, 2014

Scott-James, Anne, *Sissinghurst: The Making of a Garden*, Michael Joseph, 1975

Thomas, Graham Stuart, *An English Rose Garden: Gardening with Roses at Mottisfont Abbey*, Michael Joseph, 1991

Thomas, Graham Stuart, *Climbing Roses Old and New*, Weidenfeld & Nicolson, 1983

Thomas, Graham Stuart, *Shrub Roses of Today*, J. M. Dent & Sons, 1980

Thomas, Graham Stuart, *The Old Shrub Roses*, J. M. Dent & Sons, 1955

PICTURE CREDITS

INDEX

References to illustrations are in *italics*.

Alba roses 31
'Albéric Barbier' 110
'Albertine' 9
'Alchymist' 96
'Ambroise Paré' 2
apothecary's rose 14, 32
art 17
'Arthur Bell' 68
Astor II, William Waldorf 82, 116
Austin, David 22, 40, 110, 126
autumn damask 31, 32, 37

'Ballerina' 8, 9, 43, 44, 45, 118–19
'Baronne Prévost' 39
Bateman's, East Sussex 72, 73
Beales, Peter 22
'Betty Prior' 72
'Blanchefleur' 163
'Bleu Magenta' 96, 125, 135
'Blush Noisette' 36, 37
'Blush Rambler' 20, 50–1
Borde Hill Garden, West Sussex 75, 76–7
'Boule de Neige' 163
Bourbon roses 28, 31, 32
'Brilliant Pink Iceberg' 46–7
Broughton Castle, Oxfordshire 78, 79–81
'Buff Beauty' 40, 41

cabbage rose 31
'Camaieux' 163
'Cardinal de Richelieu' 160
centifolias 31

'Charles de Mills' 160
China 14, 18
China roses 31, 32
Clifford, Rosamund 89, 92
climbers 49, 62, 69, 170
Cliveden, Buckinghamshire 82, 83–5
'Complicata' 26–7, 148, 149, 163
Compton Castle, Devon 63
'Comte de Chambord' 37, 38, 39, 101, 125, 135
Confucius 14
'Constance Spry' 110, 111
'Cornelia' 74, 155
Coughton Court, Warwickshire 6–7, 86–8, 89–103
'Crimson Shower' 8, 9
'Crown Princess Margareta' 94

damask roses 31, 32
David Austin Roses, Shropshire 22, 106, 107–9
deadheading 49, 170
'Debutante' 115, 125, 132, 135
diseases 170–1
dog rose 28, 31, 148
'Dorothy Perkins' 64–5
Dot, Pedro 105

Eliot, George 71
English roses 40
'Escapade' 10, 11
'Evangeline' 139

'Fantin-Latour' 57, 97
feeding 170
'Felicia' 132, 155
'Fellowship' 83
'Ferdinand Pichard' 32, 33

floribundas 40
fossils 14
'François Juranville' 68
'Frensham' 72

gallica roses 32, 37, 90, 148
Garçon, Armand 94
Gardenesque 18–19
'Geoff Hamilton' 116
Gerard, John 17
'Gertrude Jekyll' 6–7, 9, 40, 41, 78, 96, 101, 102, 103
'Goldfinch' 19, 96
'Graham Thomas' 23, 58, 126, 127
Great Chalfield Manor, Wiltshire 62
ground cover roses 40
Guillot, Jean-Baptiste André 43
'Gypsy Boy' 31

Hardy, Julien-Alexandre 130
'Heather Muir' 120
Helmingham Hall, Suffolk 112–14, 115
'Hever Castle' 116
Hever Castle and Gardens, Kent 116, 117–19
'Hiawatha' 137
Hibberd, Shirley 19
Hidcote, Gloucestershire 19
Hill, Susan 27
Hill, Thomas 17
Hillings Nursery, Surrey 21, 22, 124
hips 22, 23, 24
history 14, 17–22
Hole, Samuel Reynold 18, 167
'Honorine de Brabant' 136

hybrid musks 40
hybrid perpetuals 32
hybrid teas 32, 37, 40–3, 170
hybrids 18, 21, 28

'Iceberg' 8, 9, 40, 41
'Indigo' 130
'Irène Watts' 34–5
'Ispahan' 124, 130

'Jacques Cartier' 8, 9, 37, 39
Jekyll, Gertrude 19–21, 62, 124, 163
Jellicoe, Geoffrey 82
Joséphine, Empress 17–18

Keats, John 7
'Kiftsgate' 120
Kiftsgate Court, Gloucester 120, 121
Kipling, Rudyard 73

'La France' 28, 43
'La Reine Victoria' 28
'Lady Hillingdon' 36, 37
'Lady of Megginch' 107
'Lady of Shalott' 84–5
Laffay, Jean 155
'Laura Ashley' 40, 41
Lawrence, Mary 17
'Leda' 32, 33
'Little Gem' 135
'Little White Pet' 97, 125
Lobb, William 155
Loudon, John Claudius 18–19

'Madame Alfred Carrière' 151
'Madame Grégoire Staechelin' 105, 136

'Madame Hardy' 131, 163
'Madame Isaac Péreire' 31, 94, 95, 101
'Maiden's Blush' 10, *30*, 31
Malmaison 17–18
Margottin Père & Fils 94
'Marguerite Hilling' 105
'Marie-Louise' *130*
Marriott, Michael 22
'May Queen' 160
McLaren-Throckmorton, Clare 89
'Mermaid' 160
miniatures 43
modern roses 40, 43, 170
moss roses 32
Mottisfont, Hampshire *2*, *12–13*, 21, *60–1*, *122–3*, 124–35, 148
'Mr Bluebird' *42*, 43
Munstead Wood, Surrey 21
'Muscosa' 32, *33*
musk roses 37

National Rose Society 18, 21
'Nevada' *104*, 105
'New Dawn' *49*
Nicolson, Harold 144, 151, 153, 155
'Noisette Carnée' *36*, 37
noisette roses 37

old roses 28, 32, 37, 169

'Pallida' 37
'Parkdirektor Riggers' *63*
Parkinson, John 17
partner plants 52–9, 69
Pashley Manor Gardens, East Sussex *34–5*

patio roses 43
Paul, William 18
'Paul's Himalyan Musk' *48*
'Peace' 21
Peckover, Cambridgeshire 136, *137–8*
Pemberton, Joseph 40, 44
pergolas 62–3, *64–5*
'Pergolèse' *36*, 37
pests 170–1
'Petite de Hollande' *30*, 31
'Phyllis Bide' 136
planting 168
planting companions 52–9, 69
'Plena' *144*
poetry 7, 10, 13, 73, 146
Polesden Lacey, Surrey *64–5*
polyanthas 43
Portland roses 37, 39
'Pot o' gold' *42*, 43
pruning 169–70

'Quatre Saisons' 32
'Queen Elizabeth' 9
Queen Mary's Garden, London 139, *140–1*

ramblers 49, 62, 69, 170
'Rambling Rector' 164, *165*
'Raubritter' 132
Redouté, Pierre-Joseph 17
Robin, Jay 75
Robinson, William 19, 24, 163
Romans 14
Rosa canina 28, 31, 148
Rosa x *centifolia* 16, 17, 32
Rosa chinensis 'Minima' 43
Rosa x *damascena* 31

Rosa gallica var. *officinalis* 14, *15*, 32, *120–1*, 148
Rosa glauca 96, 98, 99, 163
Rosa moschata 37
Rosa moyesii 23, 24, 25, *160*, *161*
Rosa mulliganii 68, *163*
Rosa mundi 32, 53, 88, 90–3, *120–1*
Rosa odorata 37
Rosa x *odorata* 'Mutabilis' *30*, 31
Rosa paestana 37
Rosa pimpinellifolia 28, 29
Rosa pulverulenta 14
Rosa spinosissima 163
rose types 28, 32, 37, 40, 43, 49
Rosemoor, RHS, Devon 142, *143*
'Roseraie de l'Hay' *36*, 37
'Rubra' 9
rugosas 37

Sackville-West, Vita 24, 90, 144, 146, 151, 153, 160, 163
Sales, John 124, 129
'Sander's White Rambler' *64–5*, *136*, *142–3*
Sappho 13
Scotch rose 28, *29*
scramblers 49
'Seagull' *138*
shows and exhibitions 18
'Sissinghurst Castle' 144, *152*, 153
Sissinghurst Castle Garden, Kent 20, 23, 53, 144–63
Smith, Troy Scott 160
soil 168
'Souvenir de la Malmaison' 124
species roses 28, 169

Spry, Constance 110
standard roses 62
Stud Chinas 18
'Summer Song' *84–5*
'Sweet Dream' *42*, 43
symbolism 14

Taylor, Patrick 69
tea roses 28, 37
'The Lark Ascending' *82*
'The Pilgrim' 97
Theophrastus 14
'Thomas à Becket' *84–5*
Thomas, Graham Stuart 21, 22, 124, 126, 129, 130, 132, 135, 148
Throckmorton family 89
Tollemache, Xa 115
'Tuscany Superb' 32, *33*, 160

'Valentine Heart' 72
Vass, Jack 163
'Veilchenblau' 66, 67
Vickers, Jamie 92

'Warm Welcome' *83*
weeding 170
'White Pet' *42*, 43, 56, 103
'Wild Eve' 58
'William Lobb' *101*, *102*, 156, *157*, 160, 163
Williams, Cristina 89, 101
Williams, Robin 75
Windsor Great Park *46–7*

'Zigeunerknabe' *30*, 31, 163

ACKNOWLEDGEMENTS

I would like to thank Peter Taylor and Katie Bond for commissioning me; Chris Lacey for his atmospheric photographs; Susan Hill for letting me reproduce her wonderful words; and Patrick Swan, for kindly reading the manuscript and sharing his expertise. Special thanks also to James Hellyer for his well-considered and always honest comments, and to Stephanie Mahon, Vicky Sartain and Kendra McKnight, who lent me their eyes when I needed a second opinion.

Above all, I raise my glass to all the amazing, passionate gardeners without whom we would not be able to enjoy the gardens featured in this book. My thanks go to all of them and especially Jamie Vickers, Helen Champion, Jo Jones, Troy Scott Smith, Andrew Mudge, Viktoria Gal and Jonny Norton.

I dedicate this book to my mother, for her constant support and encouragement, and to my father, who instilled in me a love of gardening at an early age, even though I didn't realise it at the time.